Museums & Archaeology in West Africa

Also published on behalf of the
West African Museums Programme
in association with the
International African Institute

Museums & the Community in West Africa
eds. Claude Daniel Ardouin and Emmanuel Arinze

Museums & History in West Africa
eds. Claude Daniel Ardouin and Emmanuel Arinze

Museums & Archaeology in West Africa

Edited by
CLAUDE DANIEL ARDOUIN

Published on behalf of   Smithsonian Institution Press
The West African Museums Programme   WASHINGTON

in association with   James Currey
The International African Institute   OXFORD

© 1997 West African Museums Programme
All rights reserved

Published in the United States of America
by Smithsonian Institution Press

ISBN 1-56098-785-5

Library of Congress Catalog Number 95-68002

First published in Great Britain
by James Currey, Oxford

Typeset in 10/11pt Bembo by Exe Valley Dataset, Exeter, England
Printed in Britain by Villiers Publications, London N3

Contents

Foreword — Emmanuel Arinze — viii

Introduction — Claude Daniel Ardouin — ix

PART I Archaeology, museum, training

1 Ghana
   Museum & archaeology training — J. R. Anquandah — 3

2 Nigeria
   The Ibadan experience to date — Bassey W. Andah — 12

3 Côte d'Ivoire
   The Université nationale & the Musée national
   An educational experience — Bernadine Biot — 24

4 Senegal
   Museography in the theory of archaeology teaching — Adama Diop — 29

5 Nigeria
   The History of the University of Nigeria Museum
   & its role in fostering research & education — V. E. Chikwendu — 37

6 Benin
   Training in archaeology
   The beginning of an experiment — Alexis B. A. Adandé — 44

PART II Museums & the management of the archaeological heritage

7 Côte d'Ivoire
When scholars abandon the people — Fofana Lemassou — 55

8 Mali
The inland delta & the Manding mountains — Téréba Togola — 59

9 Nigeria
The case of Jos Museum — Anthonia K. Fatunsin — 68

10 Burkina Faso
Museums & the archaeological heritage — Antoine Millogo Kalo — 77

11 Senegal
Towards a new policy to protect sites & monuments — Abdoulaye Camara — 81

12 Niger
The case of the Musée national — Mariama Hima — 94

13 Cape Verde
Site & archaeological heritage conservation at Cidade Velha — Nelida Maria Lima Rodrigues — 98

PART III Communication & education

14 Burkina Faso
Archaeological information, education & museums — Almissi Porgo — 107

15 Mali
Opening the Musée national to schools — Seydou Ouattara — 111

16 Côte d'Ivoire
*The value of the remains of material culture
to the knowledge of the peoples* — *Gilbert Gonnin* — 120

17 Benin
Museums & education — *Rashida Ayari de Souza* — 125

18 Cameroon
*The teaching & transmission of archaeology
in a national museum* — *Germain Loumpet* — 134

19 Kenya
Museums, archaeology & the public — *George H. O. Abungu* — 142

20 Nigeria
Museums in archaeology education — *Yashim Isa Bitiyong* — 155

Index — 167

Foreword

EMMANUEL ARINZE
Chairman, West African Museums Programme

Over the last ten years or so the West African Museums Programme (WAMP), the West African Archaeological Association (WAAA), and the International Council of Museums (ICOM), together, have been pressing the cultural actors to be more realistic and engage in multidisciplinary work. It was with such an approach in mind that, in December 1984, the WAAA convened its fourth colloquium at Nouakchott (Mauritania) to discuss two topics, one of them being the 'restoration, conservation and presentation of collections in African museums'. This approach of solidarity between archaeologists and museologists was strengthened the following May when the West African Museums Programme organized a colloquium on local museums in Lomé. There archaeologists were invited to reflect on the use of archaeological sites to build local museums. (See *Museums and the Community* edited by Claude Ardouin and Emmanuel Arinze, James Currey, 1994). Then in November 1991 it was ICOM's turn to bring archaeologists and museologists together for a brainstorming session on the topic 'What museums for Africa? The future of a heritage'.

Finally, in Abidjan, in 1993, WAMP called together a group of archaeologists and museologists to think about the most fundamental aspects of the future of African culture and about development. Our approach was dependent on our knowledge and understanding of one another and we resolved that such mutual knowledge and understanding must be increased: by including some archaeology in the training of curators and perhaps some museology in the training of archaeologists.

In Abidjan we considered the situation of archaeology and museology training in our various countries; we compared national experiences and assessed the content of courses in the various training programmes. We further discussed the need to improve communications and collaboration between the two groups.

In looking at our experiences described in this book and in keeping in mind the deliberations of our Lomé meeting (as published in *Museums and the Community*), we need to remember the results of the ICOM Colloquium of 1991 and the fifth WAAA Workshop of 1992, held in Ouagadougou. In all these meetings it is clear that training, education and communication are very important factors in any progress that WAMP and other organizations have been able to make. I trust that the national experiences described here will further WAMP's aims of helping to improve the situation for the archaeologists and museologists of tomorrow. We are determined to go forward with projects that not only bring us more together, but teach us to work together to our mutual benefit.

Acknowledgements

The organization of the Abidjan workshop from which this volume derives was made possible by the Rockefeller and Ford Foundations, whose decisive support must be stressed. Similarly, thanks go to the information service of the United States Embassy in Abidjan and to Air Afrique, which contributed enormously to the holding of the meeting. Particular thanks are also due to the team of the Musée National in Abidjan for its highly efficient support for the organization of the workshop. Special mention should also be made of the contribution of Agbenyega Adedze (Tony), of WAMP, to the coordination of, preparation for, and organization of the workshop. El Hadj Mbaye Gueye, of WAMP, assisted with the preparation of the papers for publication.

In preparing this volume for publication, the Editors would particularly like to thank Dr Kevin MacDonald, Institute of Archaeology, University College London, for permission to reproduce photographs from University College London's Thurstan Shaw Collection and from his own private collection. Thanks are also due to Professor Thurstan Shaw and Doig Simmonds for their help and comments on the beginnings of the Department of Archaeology at the University of Ibadan.

NOTE: Where photographs within chapters are unattributed, they have been supplied by the authors of those chapters.

Introduction

CLAUDE DANIEL ARDOUIN
formerly Executive Director WAMP

Are museums in West Africa destined to remain, for the most part at least, alien bodies, desperately marginal in relation to national communities and cultural worlds, or can they really succeed, as intellectual institutions, in playing an active role in the development of their societies? That question raises another: what are the issues in their development in the sub-region and, generally, throughout Africa?

One of those issues, and certainly one of the most important ones, is that of making the most of the impact of museums on public life and development as institutions working to increase knowledge and make it accessible to the communities they are supposed to be serving. From this angle, the relationship between museums and scientific research is a particularly crucial factor. In particular, the role that museums are normally called upon to play in education (and the effectiveness with which that role is performed), together with their capacity to use their holdings to communicate with their public on a range of subjects of interest to society, are dependent on that relationship. Depending on the type and level of complexity of their activities, they are users of the results of scientific research and, in varying degrees, themselves actors in that research.

What links are there at present in West Africa between museums and scientific research? Practice reveals how weak they are. With very few exceptions, museums are suffering from the inadequacy or lack of both domestic research programmes and institutional links with external researchers. That impacts on holdings – which, without the support of a systematic research effort, become mere assemblages of objects of little interest – as well as on exhibitions and educational programmes. At the same time, in each country, the results of current research are accessible solely to a narrow circle of national and foreign experts, but hardly or not at all to national publics or even to formal education. Among the intermediary institutions that could help to fill that gap, museums offer a significant potential which, to date, has been little used.

It was in the light of this situation that in 1993 the West African Museums Programme embarked on a series of international workshops on the general theme of 'Museums, research and communication'. WAMP's initiative is designed to facilitate communication by bringing museum professionals and researchers together to reflect on the relationship between museums and scientific research and the potential role of museums in education and as a medium for disseminating the results of research. The initiative envisages a

Introduction

series of programmes, each combining an experimental exhibition, an international workshop whose proceedings will be published and pilot projects. The programmes will examine a succession of topics: 'Museums and archaeology', 'Museums and history', 'Museums and urban culture', 'Museums and contemporary sculpture', 'Museums and the environment'.

The first workshop, entitled 'Museums and archaeology: the quest for public communication', was held in Abidjan (Côte d'Ivoire) on 22–8 June 1993. It was accompanied by an exhibition, 'The history of Côte d'Ivoire through archaeology', put on by the Musée national in Abidjan, in association with researchers at the Institut d'Histoire d'Art et d'Archéologie Africains. In what way was the holding of this workshop justified?

In many countries in West Africa, despite its shortcomings and the enormous difficulties that it encounters, academic archaeological research, generally conducted outside museums, has markedly enriched knowledge of local history and cultures. Major studies have been undertaken and archaeological material has been collected. However, this knowledge is generally accessible only to a few specialists. It is incorporated into school textbooks belatedly and partially. It thus remains inaccessible to the national public, since the products of excavations are still rarely put on display or used in educational courses. At the same time, the problems of preserving the archaeological heritage are exceedingly complex and made worse by the inadequacy of archaeological research and the startling spread of the looting of sites and the illicit traffic in archaeological objects.

Such a situation raises many questions. Is it justifiable and acceptable, especially in this day and age, for the citizens of a country to be kept from their own history and a cultural heritage which concerns them so closely? What relationship is there between archaeological research, access to knowledge of history and culture, the preservation of the archaeological heritage and the development of society? In each regard, what action can West African museums take as institutions? How can we envisage communication with national publics so as to make archaeological knowledge accessible to a wider audience in the country? What are the relations between museums, archaeological research, the education system and government departments? How can those relations be improved or, in countries where they hardly exist, how can they be created? How can inter-institutional exchanges in the sub-region be strengthened?

These questions underlay the intellectual approach of the Abidjan workshop, which brought together some thirty archaeologists, museum professionals and teachers from eleven African countries and the United States. The proceedings of the workshop were organized into three main panels, corresponding to the parts of this book, to deal with the main areas that needed to be tackled.

The first, Part I of the present volume, 'Archaeology, museum, training', examines the relationship between the training of museum curators and that of archaeologists, as well as relations between university departments and museums. The lack of rigorous training courses for technical staff and museum curators continues to be a serious problem in the sub-region. The development of effective links between the activities of museums and archaeology raises questions about the content of the training of future museum specialists and future archaeologists. Among other options, a multidisciplinary approach might help to create more linkage and interaction between the two fields of action.

As for relations between academics and museums, the case studies and subsequent discussions (the latter not reproduced here) bring out their full diversity, which ranges from varying degrees of collaboration to rivalry, by way of mutual ignorance. Co-operation between these institutions is enormously important for knowledge and preservation of the archaeological heritage.

Part II, 'Museums and the management of the archaeological heritage', analyses different situations with regard to the management of the archaeological heritage. The existence of specific legislation does not necessarily mean that laws are implemented in practice. In this area the action of museums remains very limited. In general terms the management and preservation of the cultural heritage almost everywhere require the introduction of a new type of relationship with national publics. It should include, among other things, a genuine communication strategy, using national languages, and the involvement of local communities in research activities and exhibitions that concern them. That cannot be separated from the adoption and effective implementation of appropriate cultural policies, very often quite different from those that currently prevail.

Part III, 'Museums, archaeology: communication and education', raises a number of questions. How can the knowledge established by archaeology be made accessible to national publics? How may school education derive benefit from it? Again, situations vary. However, apart from a few cases of substantial institutional experience, in this area there is generally agreed to be a total lack. There are simply too few archaeological exhibitions and educational programmes, for schoolchildren or the general public. As for existing activities, the problem generally arises of how national publics perceive them and above all of the difficulty (or impossibility) of their being understood by national publics, as a consequence of the inappropriateness of the intellectual standpoints (based on Western models that are themselves under challenge) and the non-use of national languages. The problem concerns museums in the first instance, but it also concerns those involved in communicating archaeological knowledge to national communities.

Another gap observed is in the use of the mass media to inform the public about the archaeological heritage. Museums must learn to use the media, while media professionals must become more interested in issues to do with the cultural heritage.

Beyond the specific questions on which they focus, the parts are interlinked, and a reading of the individual chapters provides a cross-section of many aspects. Among other things, it makes possible a rediscovery which may seem paradoxical: in West Africa some of the oldest museums owe their existence, wholly or in part, to archaeology, and to the interaction between research work and the development of holdings and exhibitions. It is, of course, quite legitimate in this day and age to criticize the colonial way of seeing things and intellectual approach. At the same time it must be admitted

Introduction

that the link which once existed between museums and archaeological research has often faded or been weakened. Is this a loss or the normal course of progress?

In any event, the crucial issues which affect the archaeological heritage today oblige us, in museums, to envisage relations with archaeologists and our national publics differently. The frankness of the discussions during the workshop demonstrated the willingness to do so and to move forward a debate which can only be beneficial to the development of museums in West Africa.

Finally, it is important to stress that the Abidjan workshop was the fruit of a particularly effective partnership between WAMP and the Directorate for the Promotion of the Cultural Heritage (Ministry of Culture) of Côte d'Ivoire.

PART I

Archaeology, Museum, Training

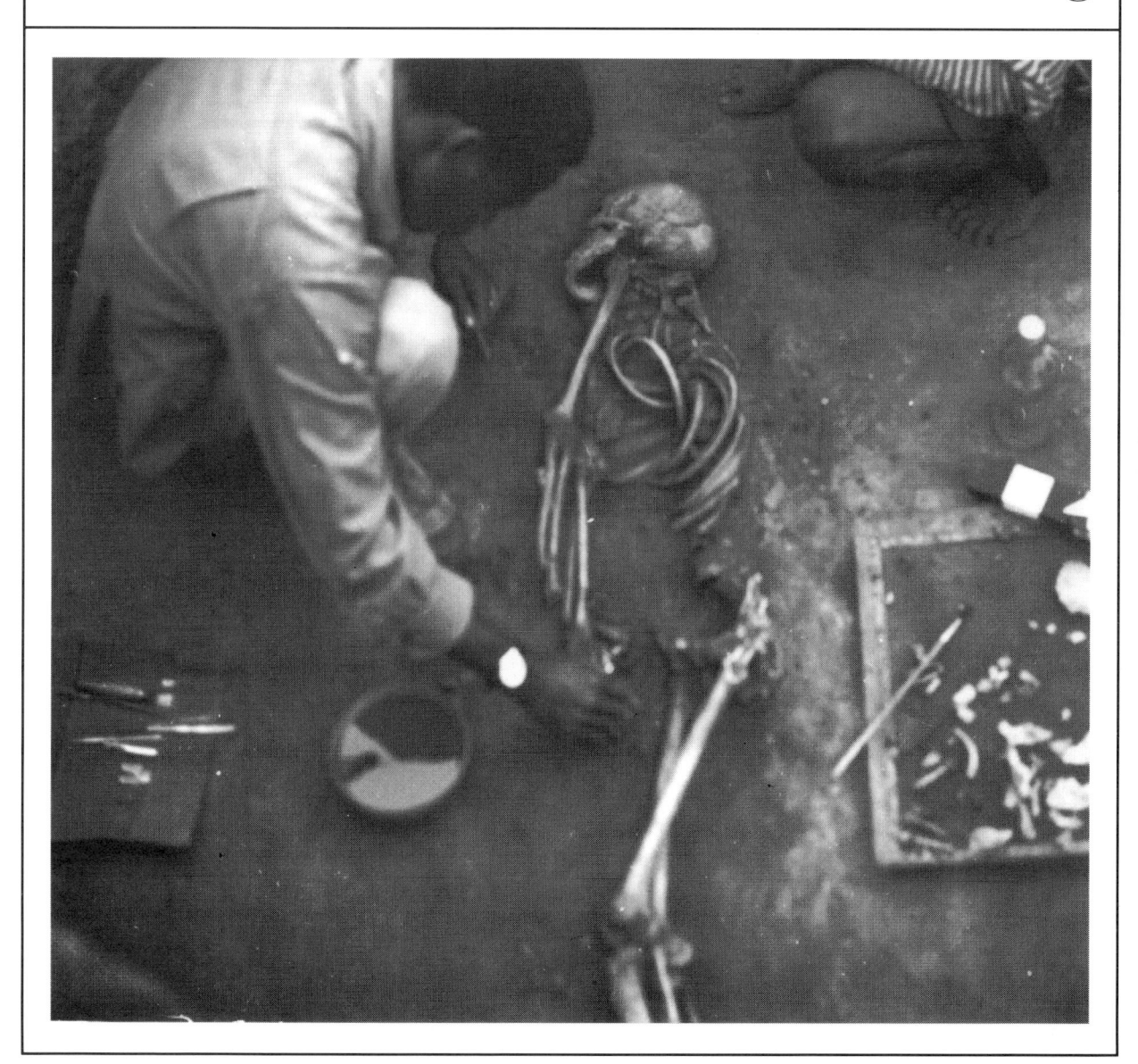

1 Ghana
Museum & Archaeology Training

J. R. ANQUANDAH
University of Ghana, Legon

In Ghana, archaeology as a pedagogic discipline promoted by research and dissemination has developed alongside the museum institution.

In the 1940s a Cambridge scholar, Thurstan Shaw, the first trained archaeologist to work in Ghana, initiated this symbiotic relationship between archaeology and museums. He is known to have carried out the first scientific archaeological excavations at Dawu, Akuapem, the Bosumpra cave, Abetifi, Kwahu, and an iron smelting site at Achimota farm. He also collected diverse ethnographic materials from different parts of the country. The data from these archaeological and ethnographic research and acquisitional pursuits were brought together as a small collection which he nurtured over the years and was to become the Achimota College Museum of Anthropology. When the Department of Archaeology was set up at the University of Ghana in 1952 the Achimota Museum collections in their entirety were transferred to Legon and served as the nucleus around which grew the future museum of the Department of Archaeology.

On the attainment of independence in 1957 the government inaugurated Ghana's National Museum at Accra and a substantial portion of the Achimota College Museum collection at Legon was transferred to the National Museum. The first Ghanaian to become Director of the National Museum had received his initial training both as a research assistant in archaeology and ethnography and as a museum curatorial assistant under Thurstan Shaw at the Achimota College Museum. From the early 1960s the Accra National Museum initiated a policy of providing Ghanaian nationals with overseas training in museum curatorship. One of the first beneficiaries of this training programme graduated at a British university as an archaeologist-cum-museologist, subsequently progressing to become acting director of the national museum.

For a decade after its inception the Department of Archaeology was almost entirely concerned with research carried out by scholars such as Lawrence, Davies, Shinnie, Ozanne and Owusu. Much of this early research took the form of rapid broad reconnaissance surveys covering most parts of Ghana and aimed at building up a fund of knowledge, acquiring artefacts for museum development, documenting vital information on historic monu-

Teaching programme in archaeology: Legon

Figure 1.1 A typical Koma-Bulsa burial mound being excavated by the 'quadrant' method

ments such as European forts and castles, Islamic monuments and Akan cult shrines, and essaying to rehabilitate such monuments (Davies, 1967; Lawrence, 1963; Anquandah, 1982).

In 1963, however, the department embarked on the teaching of archaeology with a two-year graduate programme leading to the diploma in archaeology. The sole beneficiary of the Legon diploma was the present writer, in 1963–65, after which the programme was replaced by a two-year master's programme.

In 1967 a full-scale archaeology first-degree programme was initiated, side-by-side with the graduate programme. The curricula of the archaeology programmes were designed with an essentially practical orientation, involving the teaching of archaeological site science, materials science, photography, mapping, draughtsmanship, field and laboratory conservation, skeletal anatomy, archaeological survey and excavation techniques and anthropological field survey techniques. To facilitate teaching, the department was equipped with a small-scale conservation/analysis laboratory, a photographic studio, a draughtsmanship unit and a library.

Since 1970 some 500 students have graduated from the university with honours degrees combining archaeology with another subject in the humanities. Thanks to the new course credit semester system initiated in September 1992, it is now possible for undergraduates to graduate in archaeology as a single honours degree. The problem is that archaeology and museology have very few career openings, and cannot be expected to attract many students.

Several students who combined archaeology with subjects such as geography, history, economics or sociology, etc., later took up careers in secondary school teaching. However, a small number obtained employment in the Ghana Museums and Monuments Board (GMMB) as curatorial assistants. One of them who graduated in the late 1970s is now head of the regional museum at Bolgatanga, northern Ghana. A second was the head of the Volta region museum at Ho. Both received postgraduate in-service training under the PREMA Programme at GMMB. Three other Legon graduates took up employment at the GMMB as curatorial assistants and after a few years returned to the Legon department to take the M.A./M.Phil. degree course in archaeology in 1979, and the only Ph.D. so far produced by the department. A few products of the Legon graduate programme proceeded to American and Canadian universities for further academic courses. Some are now lecturing in foreign universities. All five lecturers now teaching in the department are products of the department.

Research programme in archaeology: Legon

The Department of Archaeology has been engaged in field research over several decades. The various research programmes have been generally geared to:
  1. Unravelling Ghana's past, especially in relation to technological, social, economic, political and biological development.
  2. Understanding the processes of culture adaptation to the local environment.
  3. Discovering the reasons for cultural changes and continuities into the present so that the viable cultural traits can be selected, adapted or improved upon and used to equip society for a better future.

For the implementation of these goals, a multidisciplinary research strategy has been used by most scholars. To this end, university archaeologists have sometimes teamed up with, or called upon the expertize of, specialists such as geologists, botanists, zoologists, anatomists, linguists, technologists, anthropologists, art historians, architects, etc.

In spite of its forward-looking vision and mission, university research in archaeology has tended, for a long time, to be bogged down with academic basic research. Recently, there has been a gradual shift towards applied research in the areas of:
  1. Historical archaeology.
  2. Ethnomedical anthropology.
  3. The ethnography of traditional technology and crafts.
  4. Art/art history.

The fruits of research into these subjects tend to appeal to tourists, aesthetes and visiting scholars and so have marketable value, quite apart from their intrinsic didactic values. This accounts partly for the department's recent focus on specific research projects such as the Begho project, the Accra Plains Dangmeland project, the Elmina Fort and Castle projects, the Komaland project, etc.

Inevitably, archaeological field investigation does entail the application of some museological techniques and services in the field as much as in the home-base laboratory. Archaeologists-in-training have been acquainted with some rudiments of museum work directly related to archaeology. However, when it comes to the practical business of handling materials that need to undergo processes of conservation, preservation and restoration, accessioning, cataloguing, photographing and drawing for purposes of

Figure 1.2 Part of a terracotta sculpture of a camelier found in a Koma-Bulsa burial mound, evidence of participation in the mediaeval trans-Saharan caravan trade

Figure 1.3a Terracotta sculpture from a burial mound of the Koma-Bulsa culture of Northern Ghana (AD1300–1800). The cowrie-form calabash helmet depicted here is still in use today as a symbol of rank

Figure 1.3b Student wearing a modern example of a calabash helmet decorated with *cypraea moneta* cowrie shells

storage, publication, or exhibition, clearly there is a need for persons with specialist expertise.

With this in view, in the 1960s the Department of Archaeology had a policy of recruiting expatriate staff with museum curatorial and conservational qualifications to administer the affairs of the department's museum–laboratory–conservation–photography complex. However, the use of such expatriate museum professional staff in addition to the normal establishment of lecturing staff was found to be extremely expensive, especially where their salaries needed to be supplemented with British government hard currency. The department therefore adopted an alternative policy of giving Ghanaian nationals formal museological training at the diploma level. Three Ghanaians who had advanced-level school certificate qualifications or the equivalent and who were already employed as technical assistants in the department were granted study leave of up to two years to undertake museum-cum-archaeological studies at the London University Institute of Archaeology.

One other technical assistant with primary school leaving certificate qualifications, who was a draughtsman, was sent to the Jos Museum for a short period of training. It is thanks to such technical staff that many of the research teaching and exhibition exigencies related to museum work have been met during the past two decades.

Figure 1.4 Elderly Dangme potter creating a *Mumui* (pot used for tapping palm wine) such as have been produced in the Accra area for at least 500 years

The department's museum is operated by means of the annual research vote provided from government subvention. So far, one member of the teaching staff has been assigned the role of museum curator, as part of his normal academic duties. Since 1973, except for a break in 1984–87, the writer has handled this responsibility. The curator is assisted by the chief technician. The

Dissemination and general education programmes of the department of archaeology

Figure 1.5 Abandoned potter's workshop, last used in 1975. Tools and artefacts from this site provided comparison with Iron Age artefacts, etc. in Dangmeland near Accra

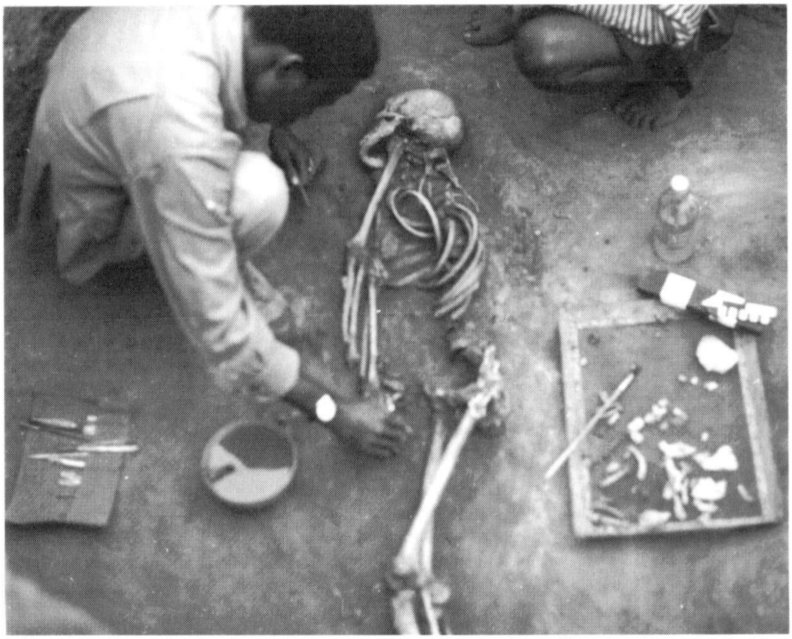

J. R. Anquandah

Figure 1.6 Ben Murey, Principal Technician, Department of Archaeology, University of Ghana (trained at the Institute of Archaeology, London), engaged in first-aid conservation treatment of a burial during an excavation at a 17th-century mausoleum at Begho, Central Ghana

museum has acquisition, cataloguing, conservation, storage and display programmes. The themes of museum displays include:
1. Human evolution.
2. Prehistoric stone technology.
3. Metal technology.
4. Craft production (e.g. textiles, beads, pottery, etc.).
5. Food production.
6. Ekistics, urbanology and State formation.
7. Art history.
8. Historical archaeology.

The display gallery is open to the university community as well as to the general public, including foreign visitors. Recently, with the launching of the new system of senior secondary schooling in Ghana, for the first time archaeology has been introduced as part of the history syllabus. The senior secondary school syllabus textbook for history includes chapters on archaeology written by the author. As a result there is now an increasing number of group tours to the department's museum organized by the secondary schools, and the department's lecturers take turns in providing a guided tour of the museum.

Relations with Ghana museums

The Department of Archaeology has close links with the National Museum and its regional centres located at Kumasi, Ho, Bolgatanga and Wa. The National Museum is responsible for issuing official permits to archaeologists

Figure 1.7 At the site of an Iron Age trading township near Begho, Central Ghana (AD1100–1800): a vertical and horizontal geodetic survey

for conducting all surveys and excavations. A clause in the permit requires that in principle a representative of the National Museum should be present at archaeological surveys and excavations for which permits are issued. In practice, however, this is rarely the case. Out of a dozen excavations the author has conducted recently, a museum representative participated in only two. It is expected that in future the staffing position at the National Museum will improve to facilitate greater participation in the department's archaeological work.

In the past, the head of the Department of Archaeology served on the board of the Ghana Museums and Monuments. Periodically the two bodies exchange personnel. For instance, the writer served in 1979–80 as an honorary keeper at the Accra National museum to help set up archaeological displays. Also, for a short spell, January 1991 to December 1991, the author acted as chairman of the Interim Management Committee of the Ghana Museums and Monuments during a crisis period.

In a number of instances, the two bodies have co-operated in organizing joint projects. For example, in 1987 the author and the director of the GMMB pooled the cultural resources of the two institutions and put up a joint stand at an international exhibition in Paris. Both institutions periodically organize seminars, symposia, lectures and exhibitions which are attended by their personnel. This ensures that knowledge acquired is shared. Currently, the two institutions are joint participants in USAID/Ghana government programmes aimed at rehabilitating selected European forts and castles and developing them as major historic/cultural heritage museums.

Monuments and archaeology

The phrase 'Museums and archaeology: training' can easily tempt one to focus solely on museums and museum curatorship *vis-à-vis* archaeology and so to overlook the equally important relationship between monuments and archaeology. Surely WAMP's aim is to bridge the gap not only between museology and archaeology but also between the keepers and conservators of monuments and archaeologists. The distinction between museology and monumentology is *not* a matter of splitting hairs, as the profession of museum curatorship and conservation is regarded as distinct from that of monument curatorship and conservation.

Tertiary institutions specializing in the pedagogy of antiquities need to develop holistic curricula that provide trainees with knowledge of museums as well as some knowledge of ancient and modern architecture, monuments and art works, and of how to conserve, preserve and curate them and disseminate knowledge about them.

The point can be illustrated by two examples. My current research focuses on two important Ghanaian archaeological sites. One of them, the Shai Hills, is an Iron Age site dated from the fourteenth to the nineteenth centuries A.D., located in Accra Plains Dangmeland and it is an urban/kingdom site 9 km by 1 km. It has domestic structures, middens, agricultural or erosional terraces, defensive earthworks and fortifications, all associated with remains of the material culture of an Iron Age people whose modern descendants are still resident in the neighbourhood. For effective research and pedagogical work on the Shai Hills, it is clear that there must be a collaborative multidisciplinary approach and team work involving archaeologists, museum and monument scholars and professionals.

The second site is a military fort, St Jago, located at Elmina. It was built by the Dutch in the mid-seventeenth century but archaeological remains have

Figure 1.8 Brass bowl bearing Islamic *Kufic* or *Nashi* inscription from Mameluke Egypt found in the ancient trading metropolis of Begho, Central Ghana. In the 19th century it was adopted by an Akan Cult shrine where it is still in use today

been unearthed from the site earlier on, as well as British cultural materials dating from the nineteenth and twentieth centuries. The research work at Fort St Jago is a multidisciplinary enterprise of archivists, historians, architects, museologists and conservators.

Conclusion

For the future the Department of Archaeology at Legon and the National Museum plan to work together more closely for capacity enhancement in the areas of research and the dissemination of knowledge and for collaborative staff training in archaeology and museum development. For example, for the new course credit semester programme launched by the University of Ghana in the 1992/93 academic year, the Department of Archaeology first degree curriculum includes courses entitled 'Elements of museum conservation' and 'Elements of monument conservation'. The curricula for these two courses were drawn up by the heads of the Museums Department and Monument Department of the GMMB respectively and they have been commissioned to teach these courses using for the practical aspects the resources of the GMMB. The inclusion of such courses in the B.A. degree course is designed to equip graduates to take up careers in the GMMB organization.

References

Anquandah, J. 1982. *Rediscovering Ghana's Past*. London: Longman.
Davies, O. 1967. *West Africa before the Europeans*. Handbooks of Archaeology. London: Methuen.
Fynn, J. K., Addo-Fening, R. and Anquandah, J. 1991. *History for Senior Secondary Schools*. Accra: Ministry of Education.
International Council of Museums. 1992. *What Museums for Africa? Heritage in the future*. Paris: ICOM.
Lawrence, A. W. 1963. *Trade, Forts and Castles of West Africa*. London: Cape.

2 Nigeria
The Ibadan Experience to Date

BASSEY W. ANDAH
University of Ibadan, Nigeria

A close relationship has always existed in Nigeria between the museum institution and the practice of archaeology both as a research and as a teaching discipline. In the case of Ibadan the Department of Archaeology came into existence with a museum attached to it. As the department developed, so also did the museum institution become more vital to its survival and growth. Indeed, if not yet in actual practice, at least in its philosophical outlook, the museum clearly constitutes the institutional homeland of the department and the effective prosecution of its programmes, the main strands of which are archaeology (cultural and environmental), biological anthropology and ethnography.

Early history of the department

The department at Ibadan started off in 1963 at an archaeology research unit in the Institute of African Studies of that university. During that early period of its history an active research team comprising mainly British archaeologists and Doig Simmonds, appointed to the post of curator of Collections, led by Professor Thurstan Shaw, laid a solid foundation for what was to become the Department of Archaeology in 1970 and since 1982 has been the Department of Archaeology and Anthropology. These founding fathers of the department successfully carried out several excavations, notably those at Igbo Ukwu (Anambra State), Iwo Eleru (Ondo State), Daima (Borno) and Benin in Edo State. While some of the material recovered from these digs went to enrich the collections of the National Museums in Lagos, others were to serve as the nucleus of the department's teaching/research collections.

Shaw appointed Dr Bisi Sowunmi to plan the palynology laboratory, its equipment and provisions. Work rooms, photographic studio and drawing office were housed at the time in the institute, as well as a display of archaeological and ethnographic materials. Shaw and his colleagues were largely responsible for designing the building complex which now houses the department, and whose central feature is an Anthropological Museum, with a range of laboratories, a photo communication unit, a drawing office, a work room and other ancillaries. Work actually began on the complex before Shaw retired at the end of 1974.

Figure 2.1 The old Institute of African Studies, University of Ibadan, where the Department of Archaeology was first housed (*Photo: Doig Simmonds*)

Figure 2.2a Iwo Eleru rock shelter at an early stage of Thurstan Shaw's 1965 excavations.

Figure 2.2b Thurstan Shaw plastering the principal skeletal remains of 'Iwo Eleru Man', in 1965. The Iwo Eleru skeleton *ca.* 11,000 bp, represents the oldest human remains yet known from Nigeria.

Figure 2.2c The impressive excavation trench of the Daima settlement mound (northern Nigeria, dating to *ca.* 600BC–AD1000) excavated by Graham Connah in 1966. (*Photos: Thurstan Shaw Collection, University College London*)

Evolution of the department's teaching programmes

At its inception the department's teaching programme had a very British outlook and bearing. Its designers saw their primary duty as disseminating information about prehistoric man world-wide, including Africa, and secondarily, providing a few students with some training in the science of archaeology, seen at the time as entailing the following: training in field surveying, excavation, artefact classification and drawing. This phase of development climaxed in the mid-1970s with various combined honours (with archaeology) degree offerings in the faculties of arts and sciences, although Shaw wisely made sure that the department belonged statutorily to the Science Faculty for budgetary purposes.

At this stage, however, a career in archaeology and museum curatorship did not appeal much to students, probably because the programme, as then structured, failed to indicate what relevance if any these disciplines had to contemporary living and the resolution if problems facing present-day man and his societies.

Reorganization of teaching programmes

A Nigerian archaeologist took his Ph.D. in the Department before Shaw retired and from the late 1970s, staff of the department, now containing quite a few Nigerians, and with the writer leading the team, began to tackle systematically the problem of making the course programmes directly relevant to present-day African societies. In this connection we determined among other things that archaeological education needed to be firmly set within a cultural frame, and in particular that of the museum and the related cultural institutions of modern society. We determined also that its primary function would be to provide the personnel of such institutions (information officers, managers of cultural resources), and planners and executors of society's development, with such training in cultural matters as would prepare them to function properly as well as to be directly useful to their societies. In other words the department established that it could not draw up an archaeological curriculum that was culturally relevant without finding out,

Figure 2.3 Temporary conservation and casting laboratory in the Institute of African Studies, University of Ibadan (*Photo: Doig Simmonds*)

first of all, what kinds of cultural institutions existed in African societies, what they did and were meant to do, and how best they could be helped to carry out their societal functions. Consequently a primary goal of the reorganization was seen by us to be that of drawing up programmes to train the cadres of cultural experts that are right for and which function effectively in modern African societies. As a first practical step we found it necessary to clarify for our purposes just who and what curators and museums are and/or should be with particular reference to the African historical experience.

Museums and museum curatorship

The term 'museum' has often been defined in a manner that reflects the peculiarity of certain countries (e.g. the United States) and also in a manner that shows even within the International Council of Museums. The search for a universal definition has succeeded only in illustrating that no such absolutely universal meaning exists, as opinion as to what a museum is and what its role should be changes with people's historical circumstances and cumulative experience. In 1974 ICOM defined the museum as a permanent institution in the service of society and its development, and open to the public, which acquires, conserves, researches, communicates and exhibits for the purpose of study, education and enjoyment, the material evidence of man and his environment.

A survey of museums in America in the 1970s ended up defining museums as institutions devoted to educational or aesthetic purposes, with staff to care for and exhibit on a regular basis the animate and inanimate objects they own or use. This definition covers art, history and science, museum technology centres, zoos, aquariums, arboretums, botanical gardens, nature centres, children's museums, park museums and visitor centres (Lurie, 1981: 181).

Both definitions point at least to the fact that a museum is a complex institution that involves interaction with collections, owners, curators and the public. But what about Africa's historical experience? Can we point to an African definition of museums? Certainly structures akin to museums are among the oldest institutions established in many African societies to stimulate the interest of certain cadres of people in the history of their societies, the natural environment and man's relationship to these (Okita, 1985). Viewed from such a truly African perspective, a majority of museums as organized and run in most African countries serve more or less as agents of underdevelopment rather than developing the good and virile aspects of the socio-cultural values and institutions of African people. Most of these museums are colonial in character and are consequently very divorced from settings and surroundings which contain vital nuclear elements of African peoples' traditions of visioning and thinking, and ways of praying, designing, planning, speaking and doing things; of organizing socio-politically and of exploiting the natural resources of their environmental settings for economic and technological ends. Important among such nuclear points have been palaces and commemoration centres, settlements of African kings and rulers, sacred groves, forests, shrine centres in compounds and larger settlements, market outposts.

In the African setting, then, it would seem that the museum was a temple as well as a forum – a vigorous meeting place where issues were discussed, where new breakthroughs in political crafting as well as domestic and industrial crafts were invented, tested and put into practice, and where those which stood the test of time were preserved, protected and improved as circumstances dictated. Thus in more senses than one the establishment of the Western type of museum in most African countries as a place for spending leisure time and for depositing exotic, not too directly useful, cultural aspects of man has been possible only through the disruption and destruction of African peoples' much more positive and quite ancient understanding of the museum as an institution. If these are some of the shades of meaning attributable to the museum concept in modern times, what about those who are charged with the responsibility of running them? What are they supposed to achieve?

The museum curator is generally considered to be a guardian or custodian who is entrusted with the responsibility of preserving and caring for museum collections (where they already exist) and making some of the collections available for public viewing in the form of displays or through other forms of public access to the collections (Okita, 1985: 79). He is the head of any museum establishment and is also referred to sometimes as the director.

The curator through his museum is meant to *acquire, conserve, research, communicate* and *exhibit,* for the purposes of study, education and enjoyment, material evidence of man and his environment. Consequently his responsibilities embrace all aspects of museum work. He is expected to be a generalist who should know a little about everything that goes on in the museum. He is not expected to be a conservator but he must know enough about conservation to be able to provide the right kinds of offices for the conservation staff. He should also be able to appreciate the rationale of spending large sums of money on humidity control in tropical conditions, although he is not expected to be a display expert.

The curator must also know enough about the effect of light on museum exhibits and about writing out labels to appreciate what can enhance the quality of an exhibition and at the same time prolong the life of the exhibits. While he does not have to be an ethnographer or archaeologist, he is expected to be knowledgeable about the requirements of field workers and about the kinds of materials field workers retrieve in order to be able to communicate their meaning to the public by exhibiting and displaying them.

He must know enough about administration to run the museum efficiently and must be conversant with the entire layout of the museum and its substance, so as to be able to serve as a museum guide, especially to visiting dignitaries, when occasion so dictates. Above all, a curator should also be involved in research, either field-based or within the museum, and concerned exclusively with the collections, with particular reference to their importance to the public that visits the museum.

While he is not expected to be an architect, he must be knowledgeable enough to brief an architect so that in the design of a museum good use can be made of natural light (Okita, 1985: 81). In European-type museums curators are often wont to suffer a crisis of loyalty towards collections as between display material and artefacts to be preserved for posterity. In our view no such crisis need arise where the curator's training is geared towards making him a manager and not just a custodian of the people's cultural resources, housed in a museum complex with excellent facilities for the preservation, conservation, restoration, display, experimentation and utilization of relevant facets of contemporary society.

X-ray of the reorganization exercise

The prime objective of the reorganization of our degree programmes was thus to make the courses more practical in outlook and more relevant to the developmental needs and aspirations of contemporary Nigerian and other African societies. The effective operation of museums in African societies was an important focus: as a result of this collective effort to contribute more actively to the quest for relevance to African societies, our programme has undergone several important changes, especially at various times through the 1980s.

First of all, by the early 1980s our archaeology programme had adopted an anthropological outlook, and a fully fledged degree course in anthropology began to be offered in addition to the new-look archaeology programme. From the mid-1980s we began to introduce cultural resource management courses. These courses, which have since been developed into an important facet of both our archaeology and our anthropology degree programmes, not only serve, together with ethno-archaeology, to link our study of past and present but also help greatly in removing the largely artificial separation between prehistoric and historical and in our bid to offer training directly relevant to museum needs.

Postgraduate programmes

At the postgraduate level, Ibadan has M.Sc. (by course work), M.Phil. and Ph.D. programmes which have been in full operation since the mid-1970s. Areas of specialization include social archaeology, ethno-archaeology, archaeological theory and practice and African archaeology. Since the late 1980s the M.Sc. and M.Phil. programmes have had the following included as specialization options: cultural resource management, conservation archaeology and museum science. The plan, which is yet to materialize for lack of adequate finance, is to build these up into full professional degree offerings.

Emphasis of the programme

Overall, our reorganized programme emphasizes the holistic interdisciplinary bio-cultural approach of anthropology. It is set within a historical and material cultural frame, while it attempts to offer two main kinds of programme: (1) specialist professional training in archaeology and anthropology, especially accentuated at the postgraduate level, (2) generalist practically oriented training in the management of cultural resources, especially accentuated in the last two years of a four-year undergraduate programme, and at the master's level.

One of the programme's principal objectives is to provide students with a range of competences which are not available in the purview of the natural or social science or history curicula but which are nevertheless crucial and needed within our educational frame if only to ascertain that development in any sector of society derives properly, as well as receiving the right stimulus and direction, from that society's cultural pool of wisdom. We are ever more convinced (as a result of actually operating the programme) that the big challenge facing societies like ours, which still suffer greatly from colonial mental altitudes, is to design and execute courses in public archaeology and anthropology (i.e. cultural resource management, CRM) which enable both teacher and students to receive the training in methods and theories of anthropological archaeology. These they require to enable them to undertake the kinds of cultural resource management project that contribute directly and positively to their people's progress and development today.

Principal aspects of programmes

As presently structured therefore, the principal features of our programmes are the training of students in:

1. The *art, science* and *technology* of building up systematically, in uniquely African museum settings, material, cultural and environmental collections, such that they can be used to address subjects pertaining to the past and present cultural life styles of a people as well as the environment they live and/or lived in.

2. The proper use of such collections to plan and prosecute relevant development projects in both a specific and an overall sense.

Apart from substantive and theory courses, as well as course offerings on Africa (archaeology, art, peoples and cultures, etc.) the main ingredients of the programme include:

1. Field training in the recovery and interpretation of cultural (especially archaeological and ethnographic) and environmental data (theory and practice courses).

2. Courses on cultural innovation, change and development, with special focus on the African cultural and social milieu.

3. Courses on material culture in society.

4. Courses in environmental and historical preservation, conservation and restoration.

The focal points of these include the treatment of grounds common to the cultural disciplines (archaeology, anthropology and museum science) and other resource-based (e.g. land stabilization) disciplines; how specialists should collaborate to protect and/or improve valued resources, as well as utilize them to promote the more efficient and healthier functioning of society; the level of public education which such experts need to provide through the results of their studies (researches).

Results of programme reorganization

Although the reorganization of the programme is relatively young it has started yielding important results. One is the noticeably greater popularity of the programmes as compared with their predecessors. Whereas through the 1970s and early 1980s we were graduating a minuscule number of archaeologists yearly (about two to five), since the mid-1980s we have been

Figure 2.4 The palace complex at Ijesha: an indigenous institution which embraces a museum. (*Photo: Akpobasa, 1991*)

graduating a steadily increasing number in archaeology (fifteen on average over the past eight years) and an average of eighteen to twenty in social anthropology. The overall number we graduate yearly will increase further when our biological anthropology is fully operational.

A majority of our graduates are now finding it easier to find an occupation relevant to their training (other than teaching). The majority of them are absorbed by the museum and related cultural institutions at federal and state level (e.g. councils for arts and culture; information, culture and social welfare agencies). Some of our products, especially in anthropology, work with development agencies like the Directorate of Rural Development and Infrastructure. A few have ventured quite successfully into the private sector as producers and manufacturers of local items and wares and as organizers and directors of tourist corporations or, in one or two outstanding instances, of oil prospecting companies.

Our postgraduate programme has been and continues to serve as an important lifeline for satisfying the staff needs of virtually all archaeology and some anthropology departments and centres or institutes of African studies in the country. For instance, of the fourteen academic members of staff at the Ibadan department, ten were trained there, most right through to their Ph.D. The bulk of the staff manning the archaeology unit at Ahmadu Bello University took their Master's at Ibadan, as also did most of the staff at the University of Nigeria, Nsukka. This list is not exhaustive and the roll call is beginning to extend beyond the confines of Nigeria.

However, we are still some way from the kind of achievement envisaged for our programmes in the long term, principally because many important facets are not yet in full operation, or even off the ground, owing to poor finances.

Figure 2.5　Ifa shrine in Ijesha Palace
(*Photo: Akpobasa, 1991*)

Figure 2.6　Sampona (Olode's) shrine in Ijesha Palace
(*Photo: Akpobasa, 1991*)

Facilities in the new building complex

With the completion of a new building complex, we now have ample and suitable space for the operation of both the department and the museum as envisaged in the restructured programme, namely an anthropological museum geared to research and the training of cultural resource officers of various kinds. The facilities include:

1. Extensive storage space (20 m×9·5 m×3·5 m).
2. Laboratories housing palynology, conservation (and to house archaeo-metallurgy when funding is available) and geo-archaeology.

3. Work rooms, one of them to house an archaeological computer unit.
4. Three exhibitions galleries. The largest (16 m×9·5 m) is designed to house the more permanent exhibitions. The other two, each about half the size of the large one, are for the display of teaching materials, the brief display of materials from on-going research work by staff, and displays of contemporary art.

Features on display in the large exhibition hall include:
1. A panoramic view of human technological history (lithics, pottery, metals).
2. The evolution of settlements in different parts of Nigeria.
3. Highlights of historical archaeological investigations in Nigeria.
4. The ethnography of some local crafts, such as basketry, pottery, beads, palm oil processing.
5. Important findings from archaeological sites excavated by members of staff past and present.

Besides a full complement of offices for various cadres of staff (lecturers, curators, secretarial) the building complex also has a drawing office unit, spacious rooms for a library, a photo communication unit with a photographic studio and space for a visual anthropology unit, field equipment and instrumentation shops, with space provided for a dating laboratory, and the offices of the *West African Journal of Archaeology*.

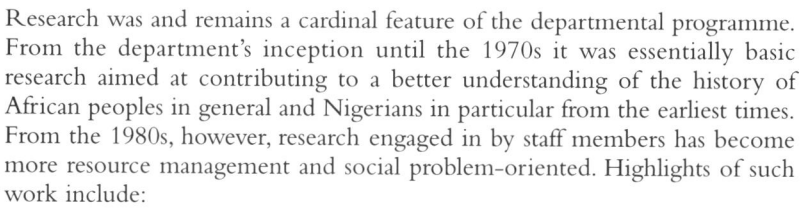

Figure 2.7 Door in Ijesha Palace complex
(*Photo: Akpobasa, 1991*)

Research

Research was and remains a cardinal feature of the departmental programme. From the department's inception until the 1970s it was essentially basic research aimed at contributing to a better understanding of the history of African peoples in general and Nigerians in particular from the earliest times. From the 1980s, however, research engaged in by staff members has become more resource management and social problem-oriented. Highlights of such work include:

1. On-going studies of the past climates and environments of Nigerian habitats and of early crop agriculture in parts of the Guinea region of West Africa, with the aid of palynology by Professor Sowunmi.
2. Long-term experimental study of the impact of environmental factors on abandoned settlements in the humid tropics, with one case study at the International Institute of Tropical Agriculture.
3. Settlement history dynamics and evolution in various parts of Nigeria (Oyo, Edo, Benue, Kwara, Niger States, etc.), with the focus on the development of towns and complex societies in African settings.
4. The development of metal technology in parts of Nigeria.
5. Ethno-archaeological study of recently abandoned Yomba settlements in parts of Ibadan, including the University of Ibadan campus.

Relations with the national museum and related institutions

Although co-operation is currently below what it ought to be, there have nevertheless been collaborative ventures between our department and the museum (e.g. the Benue project in the early 1980s), as also between members of our staff, the Nigerian museum and staff of sister archaeology departments

Figure 2.8 Slag shrines at Opi, used in museum training in reconstruction of technological development (*Photo: Okafor, 1992*)

(e.g. work at Ughuelle Uturu in Imo State in the early 1980s). In all these collaborative ventures the guiding principle appears to have been the desire to combine research with the training of students, so that maximum use was made of limited financial resources. One good idea that seems to have been born of these joint efforts was the setting up of a field school for training museologists, archaeologists and ethnographers. The aims of a field school are in fact being worked out under the auspices of the museum. Where the idea is properly nurtured and developed, such field schools could help answer the problem of time and resources available within the structural set-up of educational and museum institutions training museum curators, archaeologists and anthropologists. We also serve as perhaps the first port of call for the postgraduate training of museum staff in archaeology and ethnography.

Conclusion

What started off in 1963 as a research unit has developed since 1970 into a fully fledged department whose staff are today engaged in training archaeologists, anthropologists and museum officers at both undergraduate and postgraduate level. An important instrument for prosecuting these programmes is the museum. As part support for the work staff, members of the department have the responsibility of prosecuting archaeological and anthropological research both within Nigeria and beyond. Such research has been hampered by a severe shortage of funds, as indeed has the effective and full operation of several other facets – including basic ones – of our unique and practical oriented programme. At various times members of staff have worked in such countries as Burkina Faso, Togo, Benin, Ghana, Cameroon and the Central African Republic. Such works as well as ethnographic studies continue to constitute a ready and steady source of materials, especially archaeological, ethnographic and ethnohistorical.

Although we have a core academic and non-academic staff, all of whom are in a position to help in curatorial services, and the museum itself has ample space-related facilities, we seriously need funding and equipment to build up in such a way as to ensure the success of the unique training offered in Ibadan.

References

Andah, B. W. 1982. *African Development in Cultural Perspective*. Occasional Publications in Anthropology of the University of Ibadan. Ibadan: Ibadan University Press.

—— 1990a. 'The museum and related institutions and cultural resource management', in B. W. Andah (ed.), *Cultural Resource Management: an African dimension*, pp. 148–56.

—— (ed.). 1990b. *Cultural Resource Management: an African dimension*. Special book issue of the *West African Journal of Archaeology*, Ibadan and Owerri: Wisdom Publishers.

—— 1992. 'Cultural Ideology and Information Management in Africa'. Paper delivered at Environment and Archaeology Conference under the auspices of the Organization of African States and the US Department of Agriculture, San Juan, Puerto Rico, December.

Andah, B. W., Folorunso, C. A. and Okpoko, I. A. (eds.). 1993. *Imprints of West Africa's Past*. Special book issue of the *West African Journal of Archaeology*, 22, 1992.

Ardouin C. 1992. 'What models for African museums? West African perspectives', in I. Seralgeldin and J. Tabaroff (eds), *Culture and Development in Africa* 2.

Evans, J. 1981. 'Public archaeology and the private university in anthropological careers', in R. H. Landman (ed.), *Anthropological Society of Washington Centennial Year Essays, 1979,* pp. 42–50.

Lurie, N. O. 1981. 'Museumland revisited', *Human Organization* 40 (2), 180–7.

Okita, S. I. O. 1985. 'The curator: responsibilities, education and perspectives', in A. E. Afigbo and S. I. O. Okita (eds), *The Museum and Nation Building*, Owerri: New African.

3 Côte d'Ivoire
The Université Nationale & the Musée National: an Educational Experience

BERNADINE BIOT
Université nationale de Côte d'Ivoire, Abidjan

Since the 1987–88 academic year the archaeological unit of the Department of History of the Université nationale de Côte d'Ivoire has been carrying out an experiment in the training of young students, using the museum in Abidjan. It was initially conceived as simply to make them aware of one aspect of our cultural heritage, but it rapidly proved to be enriching for both the Musée national and the archaeological training of students because of the many problems it raised. The fact is that the museum has been stagnating, abandoned by some and ignored by others. Yet it could be an important source for research, and more particularly for archaeological research, possessing as it does an archaeological collection that is as yet intact. Many remains are stored there without the staff showing the least desire to exhibit them. What are the obstacles standing in the way of such a thing happening? Raising this question brought shortcomings in the running of the Musée national into the open and led to the beginnings of co-operation between the museum in Abidjan and the archaeological unit of the Department of History: it was a matter of seeing how far the museum could contribute to the training of our students and, conversely, how the work of these young people could help redefine the role of the museum in our society. This brainstorming led to a number of projects which we shall endeavour to present here in three main parts. The first part will endeavour to show the reasons why the Musée national has not been working as it should. The second will look at the nature of the co-operation that was launched and the difficulties encountered. Finally, we shall see how we can build on this first experience to achieve better co-operation in future.

The Musée national becalmed

Before tackling the tricky problem of the Musée national in Abidjan, we should first look quickly at the roles usually assigned to museums. That will help give us a better grasp of what is really happening in our country and understand what the approach we suggest is seeking to achieve.

A museum is above all a place where objects inherited from the past are preserved. Such remains are very varied and relate to various aspects of the life of society (fine arts, archaeology, science and technology, folk art and traditions, contemporary art, etc.). In this sense the museum can be seen as the modern repository of our material creations.

The various roles assigned to museums require skilled personnel. That makes the problem of training a subject of concern for the rational management of culture. It is therefore no surprise to find specialists in each type of collection in Western museums. Ethnologists, art historians, archaeologists, historians, palaeontologists, etc. are recruited and made available to museums as curators, and their activities are co-ordinated by a head curator. The obvious question is to know whether our museums, and in particular the Abidjan museum, are performing these various tasks. Has the museum the skills necessary to work as it should? In other words, what are museums actually doing in Côte d'Ivoire?

In the course of three years, relations with the Musée national in Abidjan have highlighted three major shortcomings: lack of a proper sense of purpose, unsatisfactory dissemination and inadequate staffing.

The museum in Abidjan, the former IFAN, was inherited from the colonial period. Its aim had been to act as a prop of colonial policy by supplying knowledge of the societies to be administered. After independence it failed to change, to give itself a different purpose: that of being the repository of an aspect of culture as the people involved see it. It was unable to establish any link between itself and Ivorian society and thus found itself at a dead end. The Musée national interests no one, and interests itself in no one. It has thus become a bureaucracy like any other and so cannot perform even its most basic task of conservation. Hardly a start has been made on an inventory (and thus little is known of what the collections actually contain), there is no real effort at enrichment, the already inadequate collection is gradually dwindling away, etc. In such conditions the Abidjan museum cannot perform any of the conventional tasks.

As regards dissemination the problem is even more crucial. Since 1981 at least the permanent exhibition has had the same features, with a subdivision into the broad geographical and cultural regions of the country. It is a silent presentation of art objects rather than a dynamic and representative exhibition. In addition, temporary exhibitions which might have made up for this shortcoming simply do not exist. And yet the Abidjan museum has the minimum holdings necessary to initiate more attractive exhibitions.

Finally, the situation becomes even more tragic if we turn to the problem of the skills of those running the museum. With a view to the wider dissemination of culture, the supervising Ministry set up a training structure intended to co-ordinate, exploit and enrich the cultural heritage. Initially it was the Centre d'animation et de formation à l'action Culturelle (CAFAC); in 1991 it became the Ecole de formation à l'action Culturelle (EFAC) but its aims are the same: to train archivists, cultural outreach workers and documentary information technicians and museum outreach workers and technicians. For this last category, with which we are more particularly concerned, the training is rich and varied. It covers both museology and law, archaeology, the history of art and the anthropology of the museum object. The students, who have the baccalaureate at least, receive two years' training and are then in theory straightaway ready for work in the field. They are assigned either to the museums as co-ordinators and technicians or to inventorying and conserving historic sites and monuments. Their presence is supposed to make the museums more dynamic and more open to the public. But that is not all that happens, since, in the absence of a complete inventory of the collections, they themselves are unaware of the museums' holdings. In addition, their knowledge of the permanent exhibition leaves something to be desired.

The experience that the archaeology unit of the Department of History has had with the Musée national in Abidjan since the 1987–88 university year led it to think about how it could help reinvigorate the latter by training students, using museum documents. An enriching collaboration has come into being.

An attempt at collaboration

Collaboration between the museum and the archaeology unit of the Department of History really took off in 1988. Originally the existence of an archaeological collection at the museum aroused our educational interest. Archaeology teaching at the Université nationale is an integral part of the Department of History. These students, future historians, receive an archaeological training which is in fact essential, given the need for archaeology to make its contribution to recovering our country's history.

This teaching begins in the second year with a course entitled 'Introduction to archaeology and prehistory', taking an hour and a half each week. In addition to field methods, the various steps to be gone through, from the excavation site to their interpretation and eventual appropriation by the museum, are studied.

For the degree, the teaching intensifies in the framework of the certificate of ancient and medieval history. Two and a half hours are devoted to general prehistory, in addition to which there is an optional one-hour course, for a total of three hours a week for our discipline. At the master's level, and for the Diploma in Advanced Studies (Diplôme d'études approfondies), we come in as required.

It should be mentioned that the setting up of the first post of full-time archaeologist in the Department of History dates from 1986. Before then the subject was taught by part-time researchers at the Institut d'histoire, d'art et d'archéologie africains (IHAAA), which failed to arouse real interest in our discipline as a career possibility.

From the beginning our concern was to complement the theoretical teaching with practical sessions – visits to the field, direct contact with archaeological material. Thus, we would offer students in DUEL II a visit once a year to the museum so as to familiarize them with the remains and documents that are held there. At the end of the outing we would take a critical look both at the exhibition itself and at the documentation. The assessment of it that was arrived at has already been mentioned above.

On the degree course, outings lasting ten days in the field were organized and students learned exploration and excavation techniques as well as how to inventory, describe and classify the material gathered.

This experience lasted three years, and from it was born a real commitment to archaeology which led to enrolments for the master's course.

As for the archaeological holding, we were informed of its existence during our visits to the museum. Among the obstacles the museum faces is ignorance as to the provenance of most objects. It includes remains from excavations and chance discoveries but it also contains other items such as lithic objects, pottery, metals, glass, bones, in large quantities. As with most other objects in the museum, there is no inventory of these remains. It is therefore difficult to appreciate their quality and quantity. The museum is at a loss as to how to make use of this holding. We have therefore chosen to exploit it for educational and teaching purposes. It has thereby become possible to offer two subjects to students enrolled for the master's degree: the study of copper alloys and the study of cultural pottery.

In addition we had wanted to cover the study of pottery material so as to establish a corpus of it and, making use of the technological advances in this area, to suggest the mounting of an exhibition on the topic. Initial contact with the museum led to a group of students embarking on the study of pottery material. Unfortunately, because of misunderstandings between the museum and ourselves, this project has still not taken off.

We should also point out that, quite separately, our colleague Guédé Yodé undertook a study of the lithic remains in this collection. The results were published in the *Annales de l'Université d'Abidjan* in 1988.

This type of collaboration is already proving to be very difficult. Sometimes research is held up by the withholding (deliberate or otherwise) of documentation. The difficulty is doubtless to be explained by the informal character of the collaboration but there is also a degree of mutual mistrust stemming from unfortunate earlier experiences between archaeologists and those in charge of the museum.

This initial contact is rich in lessons since it has made it possible to set out new guidelines for the better exploitation of the archaeological collection of the Abidjan museum.

Future prospects

The studies initiated by students and archaeologists at the museum should eventually lead to the preparation of as complete an inventory as possible of the archaeological collection. By using descriptive and analytical cards we have been able to begin the inventory, description and classification of copper alloys and today we know the various types of bracelets housed in the museum in Abidjan. The pottery collection has also been inventoried. Our aim is to prepare a documentary card index and thus identification of each item studied. In itself this record will reduce the risk of this heritage disappearing.

Further, once it knows what it has, the museum could enrich its collection by a coherent acquisition policy and put on more dynamic thematic exhibitions. From this angle the work of our colleague Guédé Yodé on stone furnishings could already be made into a temporary exhibition on the topic 'The first men in West Africa' which would include a reconstruction of the prehistoric environment, habitat and activities implied by his objects.

The problem of skills raised all through this article leads us to suggest the gradual integration of archaeologists into the team at the museum to manage the archaeological collection, as well as the establishment of research projects to enrich the collections. It would moreover not be superfluous for the museum to think about building up a multidisciplinary team if it wishes to make a success of the task entrusted to it by society. Finally, if we want the projects that have been initiated to succeed, there is a need to regulate collaboration so as to establish confidence among the various partners.

We do not claim by these means alone to resolve all the problems associated with the management of the Musée national in Abidjan. But we do think that the suggestions may contribute to a better approach to the museum collections.

The projects initiated are only in their infancy. But it is easy to see how properly structured collaboration could widen the prospects of both integrating the students we are training in the area of cultural co-ordination and rehabilitating the museum in the eyes of society.

4 Senegal
Museography in the Theory of Archaeology Training

ADAMA DIOP
Université Cheikh Anta Diop, Dakar

Applications of experimental educational methods and the advances of educational science constitute a new source of inspiration for the teaching of archaeology. As a science dealing with the study of the remains of material civilization, archaeology has a special relationship with the study of museology, which forms a natural appendage to it. The two disciplines are involved in a dynamic interaction universal in its implications, being involved in protecting the evolutionary trajectories of social groups. The evolutionist ethnologists of the last century were the first to assign intuitively an ethical function to these disciplines in the preservation of cultural heritages. These heritages, in all their diversity, are made up primarily of objects conceived by man for his survival, but also of behaviours and mental and spiritual constructs. It is a supremely symbolic atavistic legacy, which the archaeologist has to exhume and which the museologist has the awesome duty of sheltering from the ravages of time.

But the central thrust of our argument is that the evolution of the science of educational method and its impact on archaeology and museology need to be taken into account among the requirements of a methodology of elaborating and transmitting knowledge. We begin by dealing with the teaching of archaeology and its problems and then go on to the contribution of museography as a remarkable educational medium to the teaching of archaeology.

Archaeology in the university curriculum

The sacred quality of educational activity has somewhat reduced over the ages as a result of the advances of liberal philosophy. In our day, discussion of the legitimacy of education is no longer regarded as taboo, just as debate on the *raison d'être* of a particular discipline continues to be valuable.

Thus one may well ask about the legitimacy of the presence of archaeology in the curriculum of university education. Once upon a time archaeology was not taught in universities. Archaeology was attached to the Académie des inscriptions et des belles-lettres and not to the Académie des sciences, to which it is related through its various parts (geology of the Quaternary period, geography, physics), and made its mark in the resolution of the problematic of ancient civilizations. Archaeology, the science of the resurrection of the past *par excellence*, proved to be a discipline symbolizing

Figure 4.1 Archaeological excavation of the Old Stone Age site of Sébikotane, Senegal, by the author

the collective memory of peoples. It recovers the cultural norms that have fossilized over the ages; it is a strategic discipline in the awakening of consciousness and asserts a fundamental historical legitimacy when it studies the facts of civilization, reconstructing economic and social life.

However, archeology was long regarded as a scholarly, hermetic, even esoteric discipline. Its breakdown into several related sciences makes it an encyclopaedic and tentacular discipline, coming to maturity in laboratories and field excavations. The last decades of the twentieth century saw the introduction of the teaching of archaeology into European and American universities. Africa belatedly resolved to follow suit.

The organization of archaeological research in West Africa

In the first years of independence, all over Africa, programmes to inventory and study ethnic groups and their civilizations were drawn up. Africa still remained a vast natural laboratory in which anthropologists, linguists and ethnologists rubbed shoulders, giving free rein to their thinking. Whole swathes of civilization remained intact there. Yet, for many African governments, archaeological research belonged to the non-productive sector. That was a negative mental construct which in fact expressed a basic pragmatism. Is it appropriate to invest in archaeological excavations? The idea of replying in the negative, seductive to developing countries, does not confront the complexity of the question and its social and cultural implications. While economic priorities can be isolated, they must not inhibit cultural concepts, true as it is that a people which neglects its past becomes a people without a memory, culturally alienated.

The new organization of archaeological research in West Africa after independence did not spring from a root-and-branch reform. In many countries archaeology found it hard to free itself from the structures inherited from the colonial period. Belatedly an archaeological research policy was drawn up by many African governments. Generally, the legal framework is a state institution which guides what it does and defines its objectives. Archaeological research thus remains the province of a public non-profit-making enterprise.

Generally accommodated in a university, it sets itself objectives of basic and applied research on the one hand and, on the other, concerns itself with the training of future archaeologists. In some countries, such as Senegal, these tasks have been assigned to different but complementary structures, both under the aegis of the university: the Institut Fondamental d'Afrique Noire (IFAN) for field research and the Department of History (Laboratory of Prehistoric and Archaeological Research) for teaching.

This latter structure also has the task of carrying out field research through teaching workshops at excavation sites and excursions by students to the various sites. It should also be pointed out that the Faculté des Lettres et des Sciences Humaines (Faculty of Letters and Human Sciences) of the Université de Dakar has a considerable tradition of archaeological research. From 1960 to 1972 it sponsored major excavation campaigns on the medieval site of Tegdaoust in Mauritania. Rich collections were built up, a laboratory was established and several theses and dissertations were defended. Students participated actively in these early archaeological research activities.

At the Department of History of the Université Cheikh Anta Diop in Dakar the teaching of archaeology is organized within an introductory course to prehistory. It is offered to students in the second year of history and geography with a credit of two hours a week per semester. This teaching

Figure 4.2 Tegdaoust: a mediaeval stone masonry town in the Mauritanian desert, whose principal occupation dates between 11th and 13th centuries (*Photo: Thurstan Shaw Collection, University College London*)

becomes an optional unit in the third year and is offered to students who want to specialize later. The curriculum includes a course in general prehistory. This is the theoretical part, based on general methodology. A second aspect is devoted to practical work sessions on typology and various laboratory procedures. The third-year curriculum is devoted to regional prehistory.

Towards a new educational method in the teaching of archaeology

The transmission of a body of knowledge as eclectic as archaeology requires the application of a teaching method that puts the student in a situation of high-class apprenticeship. The pre-eminence of the cognitive in university education must be taken into account by encouraging the questioning of a sacrosanct body of knowledge, one that is even dogmatic in its original version. We are currently witnessing a diversification of the sources of a highly exposed body of knowledge which offers the framework for a positive confrontation and an enrichment of university teaching.

Furthermore the quality of the transmission of content remains a constant concern of the educator. A new trend in educational research advocates conceptualizing activities, leading to a hierarchical classification of clearly defined objectives. In the context of the course this means stressing the location of convincing taxonomic steps. The first objective to be assigned to the future archaeologist is the acquisition of basic concepts, using an epistemological and methodological approach. The student must first know the history of the discipline and its main methods of study. The first lectures are generally theoretical and require the use of a method that seeks to awaken behavioural reactions and attitudes to knowledge.

The first parts of the course are designed to trace the outline of the discipline and set out its problematic. The section dealing with study methods will make it possible to extend the taxonomy to applications. This part of the training is combined with regular sessions of practical work and various laboratory procedures. Here we are firmly in the area of learning know-how, methods and techniques; concomitantly the acquisition of a number of codes and languages is promoted.

Extra-mural teaching will enable the future archaeologist to become familiar with fieldwork (excavation techniques, geological prospecting and studies). Part of the course devoted to the study of the natural environment (the ecology of the Quaternary framework) will make it possible to place man and his civilizations in a spatio-temporal framework. The expository method previously used can be combined with the inductive method. This is a stage of assisted discovery, in which the use of previously acquired information combined with observation of the facts arouses a need for communication.

The most important stage in the training will be devoted to the topical study of the material remains of civilization. The archaeologist makes a veritable cult of the ancient object. This latter provokes an emotional reflex; it exercises a fascination on the subconscious of the informed observer. Psychologically, the awakening of a positive attitude must be a constant concern in the training of the future archaeologist. Here we are approaching the decisive stage in the adoption of the premises of the typology.

The first quality of the archaeologist is measured by his ability to demonstrate his expertise correctly. We are in a discipline which has suffered from hoaxes and the development of ideologies. The archaeologist must be able to decode every ancient object. The prior objectives can be listed as follows: at the end of the lesson the student should be able to identify the object, describe it, specify its function and place it in a model list. If these objectives are to be attained, the educator will have to treat knowledge as an object of teaching through the choice of an effective educational method. Archaeology is a discipline well suited to the diversification of media and the use of audio-visual and computer teaching aids to assist the observation and understanding of phenomena.

Assessment represents an important stage in training. It is no longer enough to be content with assessment by reference to a standard which requires the future archaeologist to regurgitate mechanically memorized knowledge. Assessment exercises must bear on practical applications. If the training is to be real, assessment must make it possible to test know-how. The most useful training exercises place the student in the situation of managing his own know-how, measuring it, controlling it and consolidating it through feedback on his cognitive abilities.

The coherent teaching of archaeology requires a great variety of media. Museography represents a remarkable educational method, with which we shall deal at length.

Figure 4.3 A pile of stone tools discovered at Sinthiou Bamambé, Senegal, by the author

Museography, a remarkable teaching aid in archaeology

Museography has had many avatars in Africa. West Africa has built little in the way of new infrastructure. The existing museums date from colonial times. A nasty mercenariness and slipshod management of the cultural heritage have allowed numerous objects to be transferred outside Africa. In our own day a systematic inventory of objects, hand in hand with an authenticity appraisal, would show that our museums are in an advanced state of decay. Furthermore, in countries where the Muslim religion is dominant, museums are barely tolerated or at least treated with a notorious degree of offhandedness and indifference. Muslim tradition rejects carved objects such as statuettes, symbols of memories of pre-Islamic idolatry. On top of that there are other sociological, economic and political problems which do little to promote the introduction of a coherent museum policy. Ministries of culture, when they exist, invest only trifling sums in museums. Let us have the courage to say that in Africa the museum owes its survival solely to the sponsorship and generosity of non-governmental organizations or friendly countries.

In this shabby state of affairs it can safely be said that the training of personnel (curators, technicians and guides) is relegated to a back burner. In Africa any cadre (teacher, social scientist) can do the job of curator. Everything proceeds as if museography were not a demanding science that requires specific training. The remains on which the museologist works are of such fragility that specific treatment is needed, irrespective of the complexity of the problems of restoration.

Upstream from the process of training the archaeologist, museology is a science of synthesis which seeks to bring together the scattered links of material civilization for the purposes of conservation. To that end, collaboration between the archaeologist and the museologist is vital.

The use of museography as a teaching aid demands first of all a number of prior operations. The object intended for the museum is a raw material, needing to be transformed into an object of teaching. After fieldwork and the laboratory study of the material, the archaeologist must send a number of objects to the museum. The curator and his fellow workers are entrusted with a delicate task of restoration and recovery. Every object belonging to an ancient civilization was created by a thinking mind that must be taken into account. The object cannot be regarded as having been created in a vacuum. In fact it is the end product of a whole process of conceptualization that it is the task of the museologist to ascertain. The three levels of the dialectic are present in every ancient object:

1. The need, the pre-form and the fabrication as such.
2. The object lives and fulfils its function but its end will be its destruction and fragmentation.
3. The archaeologist intervenes after several generations, digs up the object and works with the museologist to reassemble the scattered pieces.

It is vital to take this dialectic process into account in reconstituting the object and recovering its initial appearance to give it back its spatio-temporal life. The object in fact represents the coming together of a multiplicity of factors. The intimate dialogue between the archaeologist and the museologist represents an initial moment in the inventory of the problems to be resolved.

The problems of appraisal involve ever more effective scientific means (spectrography, x-rays, ultra-violet and infra-red rays; crystallography – mineralogy, physical dating methods, etc.). The museologist must steep himself in this scientific environment. The second stage of the training concerns the laboratory techniques applied to reconstruction, restoration and recovery.

Discoveries of complete objects are rare in archaeology. Generally they are found mutilated, incomplete and scattered over the site. Some parts of them will never be found. The museologist must first be trained in *reconstruction*. This is the operation that consists of identifying and assembling the pieces that have been preserved. Reference to our previous dialectical conceptualization of the ancient object, discovered in pieces by archaeologists, will show that the concern for reconstruction is obvious. A good reconstruction must be based on the physical state of the pieces, the traces left by the vagaries of the elements and the direction and nature of breaks. In addition, the techniques used in making and shaping the object, the peculiarities of the raw material and the stylistic and aesthetic inspiration of the creator all have to be analysed. There may have been a significant chronological gap between the discovery of two fragments. A presumption that they are part of the same object must not be ruled out *a priori* if the two fragments come from the same site. The consistency of the direction of joins must also be taken into consideration.

The stage of *restoration* represents a significant moment in the training of the museologist. It is rare for a museum object not to bear the marks of restoration. The broad principles of a general methodology can be an inspiration, but restoration is a job that is usually entrusted to laboratory technicians. It is a work of synthesis that makes it possible to put the object together again by assembling the pieces in a coherent way. The last stage of the study of the ancient object, its end, is the *rediscovery* of the complete original appearance. Recovery may be graphic or modelled. But in any case it has to reconcile the aesthetic concern of the curator over how it is presented (finding a permanent home for it, deciding which media to use) with that of the archaeologist, who always regards the object as an archaeological document the appearance of which can be questioned in the light of scientific research.

Museographical activity comes just at the right time to help the teacher in several disciplines. The conception of a slide show in an ethnographical museum is useful in the teaching of history, art and archaeology. But the success of such a document involves resolution of the problems of picture-taking (cf. Diop, 1981). Indeed, the course can be conceived in the museum itself. On this point a certain amount of preparation is called for. The teacher can prepare a guidebook with his students. A number of aims must be sought:

1. To develop in the student an attitude of respect for the ancient object, as an element of a cultural heritage.

2. To make the student independent through acquiring skills by developing the taste for personal observation. There are a number of prerequisites: knowing how to draw a sketch or a map, how to establish a chronology, how to take notes, etc.

3. To develop knowledge (the sequence of events, getting to know how objects are made, knowing what they are for). The teacher will have to avoid clichéd guidebooks.

Another educational interest served in preparing a guidebook lies in the multidisciplinary character of the project. Disciplines such as the natural sciences (geology, biology) can be included along with history and geography. A visit to a natural history museum can be planned as a cross-disciplinary exercise through co-operation between teachers. The student is put in a learning situation which sets knowledge before the concrete. Asking the teacher questions is vital. The teacher must aim at observation, description, analysis, reflection and the development of a critical attitude. Museography can introduce remarkable educational moments in teaching by restructuring communication and diversifying learning situations.

Training in the craft of archaeology constitutes a cognitive learning process the various educational paradigms of which remain a subject of controversy among different universities. The transmission of the content of a discipline as eclectic as archaeology assumes the use of a cross-disciplinary language built on precise operational objectives. In this area experience suggests that the discursive approach of traditional educational communication should be enriched by specific training courses. Africa is notoriously far behind in the training of its archaeologists. The quantitative and qualitative shortcomings of training are obvious. 'What sort of training policy?' is one issue raised, but so too is how to adapt training to the latest advances in educational research. More than simply a subsidiary discipline, museography today represents a remarkable educational medium in the training of archaeologists. Such training requires an integrated multidisciplinary approach to awaken in the student positive behavioural reflexes towards the symbol-object of material culture.

Reference   Diop, Adama 1981. 'Etude photographique d'une industrie lithique acheuléenne: optimisation des conditions opératoires', *Notes africaines* 172, Dakar: IFAN.

5 Nigeria
The History of the University of Nigeria Museum & its Role in Fostering Research & Education

V. E. CHIKWENDU
University of Nigeria, Nsukka

Those acquainted with the physical structures of the University of Nigeria will know that there are other museums within the university apart from the University Museum. These other museums are located in the Institute of African Studies (Ethnology), the Zoology Department (Natural History) and in the art gallery in the Department of Fine and Applied Arts. Each of these museums is specialized and (apart from the Institute of African Studies museum) serves training/teaching purposes for the different units. The museum located in the Department of Archaeology assumed the ambitious title of the University Museum because its founder, Professor D. D. Hartle, envisaged that in the future it would expand and serve the wider university community and beyond. Hartle's prediction has come true. Records show that from 1988 to 1991 the University Museum became a focal point for tourists, educationists and their students, cultural enthusiasts, organizations, town unions, clubs, etc. The university administration under the former Vice-chancellor, Professor Chimere Ikoku, using the Public Relations Unit, made the University Museum its most important port of call for VIPs.

As mentioned, there are three other museums. In 1989 a call for memoranda on cost-saving methods in the University of Nigeria offered the present writer an opportunity of making a case for the unification of all the existing museums under one roof at the University Museum. The reasons for the suggestion are:

1. *The availability of a great deal of space* which will be made available when the academic wing of the department moves to the new faculty block.

2. *Administrative efficiency.* Each of the museums engages the high, medium and low-level manpower needed for its smooth running.

3. *Research and tourist convenience.* Pooling the resources will make larger and more diverse material available to researchers and tourists alike, thus attracting a higher-level clientele.

4. *Cost effectiveness.* Products and equipment needed for museum work can be purchased centrally and the activities put under the supervision of trained personnel (curators).

5. *Security* will be better and more easily enhanced when all the materials are housed under one roof.

Many other suggestions were put forward, but no reaction has been received yet.

The History of the University Museum

The Hartles joined the service of the University of Nigeria in 1963. Donald and Janet Hartle were both anthropologists, the former specializing in cultural and the latter in social anthropology. Husband and wife could not both join the same department, as it was forbidden by the university statutes. Janet opted to join the Department of Sociology/Anthropology. Donald Hartle first had a brief honeymoon with the Faculty of Physical Sciences, where he was given laboratory space in the Carver Building. He began to build up a laboratory for archaeology and soon his field reconnaissance began to yield cultural material for the storage and display of which he needed space. He therefore entered into discussions with the powers that be and obtained some concessions, including the whole of the building designed as the university laundry. One of the conditions was that the archaeology unit should move to the Department of History, which then assumed the title Department of History and Archeology. This name remained from 1964 till 1981, when the two disciplines emerged and Archaeology became a fully fledged department.

When Hartle moved to his new building he discovered that he had more space than he needed immediately. But he knew that future expansion would take up more. To occupy the space effectively, he demarcated it into a museum space and a laboratory space. Throughout 1965 and 1966 Hartle spared no effort in filling the two. Ethnographic materials were purchased to help fill the museum space, while intensive and extensive fieldwork brought in a bounteous harvest for the laboratory space.

The Nigerian civil war and its effects on the museum

Unfortunately the university town of Nsukka was one of the first locations to fall to the federal troops during the Nigerian civil war (1967–70). Because materials housed in the museum and laboratory was essentially Igbo, the occupying federal troops carried away many and destroyed more.

In 1966 Hartle had completed the excavation of the Ukpa rock shelter Afikpo. The materials had been brought in by early 1967. In June Hartle left the University of Nigeria, Nsukka, for home. While he was still in the United States the Nigeria–Biafra war broke out. Hartle was unable to return to Nsukka at the end of his leave.

As the war dragged on Hartle made a brief sojourn at the University of Lagos, waiting for the war to end. In 1969 he was able to travel in the company of federal troops to Nsukka, where he found sorted material all upturned and mixed up. His field notes, diagrams and photographs were either missing or destroyed. He managed to retrieve some bronze bells (Ifeka Garden bronzes from Ezira, near Igbo Ukwu). He claimed that he passed them to the then Resident of Nsukka, who had a breakdown at the close of hostilities and therefore could not account for the bronze objects entrusted to his care. This issue harassed Hartle throughout his stay at the university as the deans and heads of department continued to question him about the objects.

After the cessation of hostilities in 1970 Hartle eventually returned to the university. He had to face two enormous problems. The first was infusing order into the jumble that the laboratory materials had been reduced to. The second was the restocking of the museum, which had been selectively plundered. To solve the museum problem, Hartle employed students during the long vacations to scout around for cultural materials from the then East Central and Cross River States. The bulk of the holdings in the University Museum today comes from the Igbo and Afik-speaking areas of south-eastern Nigeria.

In 1971 Hartle directed the present writer (by then a student in the Department of History/Archaeology) and Godwin Odoh (a technical assistant) to erect replicas of Southern and Northern Igbo house types inside the museum. This presented some architectural problems, as the floor of the museum is made of solid concrete. To make the foundations, we had to either bore holes in the hard cement floor or make a superficial structure on which the foundations could be built. We chose the second option. Logs of wood were brought from a nearby forest and placed on the concrete floor. Vertical poles were inserted in these beams and the whole framework was thus constructed. The *domus in domo* could be moved, since the base was not permanently fixed to the floor. The southern house type had a raffia mat roof, while the northern type had a grass roof. The former was oblong in shape, while the latter was almost round. Inside each house were displayed cultural materials characteristic of its area. The completed structure attracted much attention among the university community. At the opening ceremony the museum was recognized as the University Museum.

Because of the number of visitors, Hartle found it difficult to combine his academic responsibilities with the running of the museum. This situation compelled him to engage a curator to oversee the museum and laboratory. The new curator proved equal to the task and, soon after, many visitors were thronging the museum. For the first time, opening hours were extended beyond the official working day, and included Saturdays.

University of Nigeria Museum: fostering research & education

Dealing with the museum after the civil war was easier than returning the laboratory to a state of order. The bulk of the material was artefacts from the Afikpo, Ezira and Obukpa excavations. We know that every archaeological excavation is a form of 'destruction', but destroying catalogues, field notes and drawings is catastrophic. First the tons of material from Afikpo (mainly quartz artefacts and pottery) had to be sorted out. Clearing the mess took several months. No new material could be brought in while the chaos lasted. It was only in 1975 that an appreciable quantity of excavated material could be brought into the laboratory space. From that date, excavations in south-east Nigeria accelerated, bringing in new display material for the University Museum.

The laboratory section

From 1975 till 1979 the Department of History/Archaeology was engulfed in bitter internal wrangling, with Hartle at the middle of it. Successive heads of department (all historians) who at times served as Deans of Faculty, ensured that Hartle had no respite. No effort was spared in 'getting at' him. For instance, the personal secretary who had been attached to him was removed; he was ordered to obliterate the title 'Director' on his door. The

Departmental friction and its negative effects on the University Museum

39

curator was ordered not to take his orders from Hartle (who was head of the archaeology section) but from the head of department – a historian whose office was located far away from the archaeology building, and who had no training or experience in running a museum and an archaeological laboratory. The budgetary provision for running the museum was taken away. In 1979 Hartle finally bowed out of the 'battle front', retired rather prematurely and returned to his native United States.

One would have thought that unsavoury measures designed to incapacitate Hartle would have been rescinded when he was harassed out of the system. But this was not to be. The two Nigerian archaeologists who by then had joined the department were not spared Hartle's agonies. During this period of hostilities the University Museum became neglected. The number of visitors dwindled. Since there was no vote for the upkeep of the museum, no new chemicals or adhesives were purchased. Bio-deterioration set in. No other option was left than to fight for a separate department of archaeology.

Eventually our request for the creation of a separate department was conceded by the university administration. It was approved that the department should be set up, to start operating by the beginning of 1981/82 academic session. This decision had positive and negative effects on the fortunes of the University Museum. On the positive side, there was now enough budgetary provision. There was enough money to purchase chemicals and reagents. Display platforms were built and materials were once again treated by the curator and her team.

On the negative side, we were too engrossed with setting up the academic arm to devote enough time to the museum. Also, the need for classroom space compelled us to partition part of the museum space. The museum area was therefore replanned and the new arrangement became more compact and aesthetically more attractive.

As we were settling down to tackle the museum section, the curator, also a US citizen, fled the country in 1982 for personal reasons. No handover note was available. We were still dazed by this development when the financial situation in Nigeria deteriorated in the 1984/85 session. Funding became slim again. In fact as head of department I spent the greater part of the period 1985/88 justifying the relevance of my discipline to national development.

The museum village

In 1985 our budgetary provision had gone down so much that it became imperative to look for other sources of income for the department. Apart from justify our existence, it became necessary to show that archaeology is for the living and not for the dead. I began to toy with the idea of extending the museum to the outside. The *domus in domo* which we constructed inside the indoor museum was removed when we constructed a classroom from the museum space. There was a large expanse of space east of the departmental building and it immediately occurred to us that it could be utilized for erecting bigger traditional house types. This project had become urgent because of the speed with which traditional architecture was disappearing from the rural setting in south-eastern Nigeria. Euro-American and Arabic architecture has almost replaced the traditional mud-and-thatch houses in the region. Most township-born children have lost touch with these traditional house forms. Additionally, when completed the project would serve as a tourist centre.

The original plan was to create two sections – (1) a recreational unit and (2) a traditional Crafts and Industry unit. After the approval of the plan by the departmental board, work began on unit (1) in February 1986. With departmental support, we began to erect a 235 m long perimeter mud wall. Apart from being part of the traditional set-up, the compound wall would provide protection for the structures to be erected inside. By June 1986 the compound wall was ready. At this point it was prudent to involve the university administration.

It was clear from the outset that the department did not have the resources to fund the project. However, it would be easier to get some support if we had a structure ready before requesting help. The help came, albeit in bits. The faculty also lent us moral and financial support.

The structures were set up and by April 1988 the recreational section was complete. This unit comprised a kitchen and service area, an open space for performance and a cluster of eight round huts. The largest of these was named the 'conference hut', in which we later entertained university guests. Trees were reminiscent of the village environment.

The indoor museum

At the same time the indoor museum had to be improved. There was a serious question of security: staff and visitors passed through the museum to reach the general office. So there was no distinction between a passer-by and a visitor to the museum. This situation encouraged pilfering. Given the faculty's decision to open the museum complex during the faculty week celebrations of 1988, it became urgent that the indoor museum should be given a face-lift. The university administration provided funds for the work. First of all, the thoroughfare between the laboratory area, the museum and the general office was blocked. An artist was hired to do some mural paintings. Display boxes were provided. The floor was decorated as well.

Services to the community

Official guests. The most important patron of the museum complex was the university administration. No important university event took place without involving the University Museum and museum village.

Groups. Many organized groups patronized the museum village and the indoor museum. Meetings are also held in the round huts. Town unions and co-operatives use the facilities. A wedding ceremony has taken place in the museum village. The Rotary Club held its picnic there. Film shooting requiring a village background took place after minor additions. The Children's Centre group visits the museum yearly and there is a follow-up with excursions to archaeological sites in and around the university town of Nsukka, i.e. Ogbodu Aba, Lejja, Umundu, Aku, Orba and Opi. University students' social activities are not left out. The Kegite Club (the palm wine drinkers' club) had its permanent base in the museum village. Some prayer ministries held their meetings there too.

Services to education. Colleges of education, secondary schools and some primary schools visit the museum. Once the letter of request has been received appropriate arrangements are made for hosting them. A lecturer or a technical assistant is detailed to conduct the group round their areas of interest.

Training archaeologists: postgraduate programme in museum studies. The Department of Archaeology has a postgraduate programme of museum studies. With co-operation from the staff of the National Commission for Museums and Monuments (NCMM), Enugu, we successfully produced three master's degree holders in this area. One of the recipients is already working in the Cameroon Republic. Undergraduates of the Departments of Architecture, Fine and Applied Arts and Music make extensive and intensive use of the museum. Students of architecture travel all the way from Enugu to study the traditional architecture in the museum village. Students of fine and applied arts come to do their practicals – drawing objects displayed in the museum. Education students come to borrow cultural material for use during their teaching practice.

Outreach activities. Some secondary schools have approached us requesting technical assistance in setting up mini-museums, e.g. the girls' secondary school at Isienu.

We have some priorities: a dire need to create outdoor museums at Ogbodu Aba and Lejja. The main feature at Ogbodu Aba is a scatter of 'catacombs' – subterranean structures which were used to 'house' the dead. Many grave goods accompanied the dead. This site was discovered virtually by bulldozers, located near a stream. Preliminary studies show that important dignitaries were buried in the 'catacombs', with their offensive weapons laid out beside them. Their heads were placed in a pottery bowl. The cavity was then heavily smoked and a slab placed over the top of the vertical hole.

Lejja lies about 20 km south-west of the university and is equally fascinating. The local people had dug out and arranged bucket-size cylindrical lumps of slag in rows at the village square. These slag cylinders now serve as seats for village meetings. Excavations have shown that the slag resulted from the iron-smelting activities of ancient people. Some of the slag cylinders in the vicinity are still lying *in situ* where they were formed. These two sites merit attention as potential site museums.

At present our priority is to develop our museum programmes in the following areas, in collaboration with possible partners and sponsors: (1) site development – Ogbodu Aba and Lejja, (2) rehabilitating the museum village, and (3) erecting the second phase of the museum.

Conclusion

The relationship between the museum at the University of Nigeria and the wider public is developing. The days are going when people derided the museum collections and saw them simply as objects of fun. This new consciousness of the value of our cultural heritage has its own problems. Antiquity traffickers are inducing young people to steal precious cultural material from shrines, individual collections and museums. Such deals bring in an appreciable amount of money. The University Museum was hit five times between 1989 and 1990. Valuable material was lost. We had to engage the services of two security guards.

We are all involved in the retrieval and preservation of cultural materials. We have a common interest in establishing and running museums. Departments of archaeology can help train museum personnel, while curators can help minimize losses in the field, the laboratory and the museum. Outreach programmes can be tackled co-operatively, particularly in the area of establishing and running new units. We must do something in the area of publicity.

Some people are completely ignorant of what we do. This general ignorance of our relevance to community development is reflected in the marginal budgetary provision for cultural matters, particularly in Nigeria. I was told by one commissioner that 'culture' is not on the government's priority list. At the same time museums hold important key information about how our people lived and coped with their social and environmental problems.

By studying our forbears' cultures we can decrease our exposure to Western education. We have a duty to stop the spate of spurious contracts for white elephant projects rampant in the West African sub-region and to educate our people on the need for an inward search for the solution of our problems. In this regard, cultural resource management stratagems are invaluable in stressing which aspects of our traditional life are relevant today and therefore need to be carried forward.

6 Benin
Training in Archaeology: the Beginning of an Experiment

ALEXIS B. A. ADANDÉ
Université Nationale du Benin, Abomey–Calavi

When, five years ago, the Department of History and Archaeology of the Université nationale du Bénin was celebrating the tenth anniversary of the formation of the Equipe de recherche archéologique béninoise (ERAB, the Beninois archaeological research team), it provided an opportunity to draw up a balance sheet of the efforts of each of the team's members to ensure, with modest means, the establishment of a new discipline in the context of the Republic of Benin (Adandé and Adagba, 1988).

Today, after providing teaching in prehistory and protohistorical and historical archaeology in the framework of training historians, the department has decided to try out an archaeology option to meet a demand for further training in this discipline. This chapter deals with that on-going experiment.

First we briefly review the story of the establishment of archaeological research in the Republic of Benin, then we set out the teaching and research programmes in archaeology in the university, and finally we look at the problems and prospects of specialized training in Benin taken in its regional environment.

Historical overview

When the Université du Dahomey was set up in 1970 a history section was formed in which a French technical assistant taught prehistory and Greek and Roman antiquity for a few years. Then, at the request of the academic authorities of the time, Professor Jean Devisse of the Université de Paris I, on the occasion of teaching assignments at the Université nationale du Bénin in 1975 and 1977, put forward the broad outlines of a policy for archaeological research in Benin. It fell to our colleague François de Medeiros, then head of the Department of History, to lay the basis for this research by organizing a core of researchers who formed the Recherche archéologique béninoise team in 1978. Since then introductory teaching in archaeology and prehistory and courses on topics relating to various periods from the most ancient to the dawn of history have been based on archaeological data (Adandé and Adagba, 1986).

In tandem with teaching, research programmes in archaeology have been carried out within the financial means available. The opening of a few work sites in the Mono valley at Ouidah and Savi and at Ouessé enabled the most motivated students to go on field trips. Thus a few students chose to do their master's theses with an archaeology option.

The first thesis with an archaeology option was defended in 1992 and was on the topic 'Oral tradition and archaeology: ironworking in eastern Borgou'. More recently a student from Niger presented a 'Typological Study of Lithic and Pottery Material from the Houngbanou Site (Sè, Department of the Mono, Republic of Benin): archaeological excavations in October and December 1991'. Other theses are under way on a variety of topics.

More and more students in history are including archaeological research as a means of enriching their quest for historical documents. This latter aspect legitimizes the original direction given to the teaching of archaeology in a history department. For periods earlier than the nineteenth century, oral sources, the main basis of historical documentation in sub-Saharan Africa, need to be more coherent, to rest on or to be backed up by the sort of tangible data that only archaeology and related disciplines can provide. The issue will soon arise of developing an 'archaeology of the colonial period', since even evidence from this recent period is getting weaker or disappearing altogether with development projects or unchecked urbanization. Thus it was to meet a demand for further training in archaeology that the department decided to open an archaeology option on an experimental basis from the 1992–93 academic year.

Evolution of archaeology teaching programmes

Archaeology teaching was introduced into the first cycle of the history course in the form of an introduction to the methodology of the discipline of archaeology and prehistory. Starting in 1985, a degree course was devoted to topics such as 'The Iron Age in Africa', 'Production societies from the late Stone Age to the early Iron Age'. A research seminar was added to this optional course in 1986–87 with a discussion of the topic 'Archaeology and history of cultures in Africa'.

Inter-university exchanges made possible by grants from the AUPELF (Association of Wholly or Partially French-speaking Universities) enabled colleagues from the Université de Ouagadougou (Burkina Faso) to help in 1988 and 1989 in consolidating the training of future historians at the Université nationale du Bénin. There is no doubt that this broadening of horizons stimulated interest in more specific research in archaeology in some of our students. Also, recourse to the expertise of our colleagues at the University of Ibadan (Nigeria), particularly for carrying out a programme of archaeological research in the Mono valley, put a number of our advanced students in touch with experienced researchers. The same happened with the Historical Archaeology Project at Ouidah and Savi, carried out as a co-operative venture with the University of California at Los Angeles (UCLA) in 1991 and 1992. Exchanges of students and teachers between the Université nationale du Bénin and the Université du Bénin (Togo) were on a reasonably regular footing before the recent political events in Togo.

At another level, our working relations with museums are developing favourably, particularly with the Musée ethnographique at Porto Novo. With

Alexis B. A. Adandé

Figure 6.1a Floor of brick and terracotta tiles being cleaned (likely area of European trading posts, 17th to early 18th centuries) at Savi, former capital of the Kingdom of the Houéda, destroyed in 1727

Figure 6.1b. Cleaning the exposed paving, Savi, 1994

Figure 6.1c Close-up of paving, Savi, 1994

the permission of the Directorate of Cultural Heritage, which is administratively responsible for the national museums, the ethnographic museum has made a room available to the archaeological research team of the Department of History and Archaeology. This room will house the practical work and the study material previously kept in the homes of researchers for lack of space on the Abomey–Calavi campus or in other buildings at the university (Adandé, 1992b).

Conditions are thus quite promising for the introduction of an archaeology training option. This matter was high on the agenda of the fifth colloquium of the West African Archaeological Association in Ouagadougou. The conclusions and recommendations of the colloquium on the subject of training are substantially the same as those of the teacher-researchers in my department. They are particularly concerned with ensuring there is a four-year course with an archaeology specialization from the third year, and with making that training both technical and practical while setting it on a solid historical basis, so as to address the needs and constraints of archaeological research in West Africa.

Thus a common core in the first cycle includes an introduction to working methods in archaeology and regional prehistory. In the third year (degree) students opting for archaeology must, in addition to the three compulsory courses in history (history of art, Roman antiquity and the black African diaspora), take a course in archaeology which in 1993 was on 'Archaeology and the urban phenomenon in pre-colonial Africa', and two subsidiary introductory courses in linguistics and anthropology or botany and geology. A compulsory field trip to an excavation site is also proposed, or surveying and practical work sessions on the study and handling of archaeological material. In the fourth year (second cycle and master's degree) a history research seminar is held. Although the experiment is starting out under apparently favourable academic omens, major problems still remain.

Problems and prospects

A sound training in archaeology presupposes the existence of a minimum standard of working conditions such as a documentation centre equipped with reference works and access for students to documented archaeological collections, with the possibility of participating in research work in the field (surveys, exploration, excavations). This last point poses the question of a sustained policy of archaeological investigation following coherent medium and long-term programmes, and the problem of equipping laboratories for analysis and dating.

The members of the Béninois Archaeological Research Team (ERAB) are conscious of these requirements of research and teaching in archaeology and, with the help of scholarly inter-university exchange agencies, as well as through their personal efforts, have patiently built up a documentary collection, part of which is deposited at the Documentation Centre of the Faculty of Letters, Arts and Human Sciences (FLASH) and the rest will be used to mount a small specialist library for second-cycle students in archaeology.

Alexis B. A. Adandé

Figure 6.2 Members of the joint team of Americans (from UCLA) and Béninois (from the Université National du Bénin) at the end of a day's dig, Savi, 1994

The problem of organizing the compulsory practical course is the hardest one to resolve in the absence of a budget line earmarked for archaeology at the university as exist in research or cultural heritage preservation institutions. In the Republic of Benin all archaeological activities have been carried out with external funding. That is doubtless one of the great weaknesses of archaeology in Benin. Thus, while seeking to alter a situation that is, in the long run, unfavourable to the continuity of effort in this area, the staff of the department and the team are trying to make the most of bilateral and multilateral co-operation in the area of archaeology. Thus in every field agreement or campaign a training aspect is included which involves the participation of students in research. Similarly, we are trying to make visiting national museums a compulsory part of the training of history and archaeology students. The ideal would have been to have available on the campus spaces for the study, restoration and display of a significant portion of the products of our research. As an alternative we have the co-operation of the Musée ethnographique mentioned above. This solution has the advantage of bringing us closer to the museums and the people working in them, while enabling the Musée ethnographique to build up the leading public archaeological collection in Benin once the material studied and documented has been transferred.

Finally, we are concerned about the question of career prospects for our students in a social and economic context marked by structural adjustment programmes and liberalization. Despite an obvious need on the part of our national museums and research and teaching institutions for high-quality researchers and well trained technicians, the Béninois government has stopped recruiting permanent staff since 1986 and there is much talk of redundancy in the public sector. Natural or 'voluntary' retirements are

Figure 6.3 Museum personnel who mounted a temporary archaeological exhibition (entitled *La Terre aussi est notre livre d'histoire*, together with a group of visiting teachers outside the Musée ethnographique in Porto Novo

increasing the shortage of staff in our museums and depriving the inventory department of senior and supporting staff. But a system of temporary recruitment of young unemployed graduates has been instituted to fill the most dangerous gaps, while tourist agencies are developing which may eventually absorb some of the archaeology students who will be entering the labour market in two or three years. (In 1993 only four chose this option.)

It is impossible to draw up a balance sheet of the archaeology training course, an option which has only just got off the ground at the Université nationale du Bénin. On the other hand the introduction to archaeology, which has been available for almost fifteen years as part of the history training, has begun to bear fruit in the form of a real interest on the part of a growing number of young researchers in this discipline and its irreplaceable contribution to the documentation of large periods of the past of Africa in general and of Benin in particular. The introduction of an archaeology option within the Department of History and Archaeology answers a need, felt in most universities and countries in the sub-region, to train researchers and technicians of sufficient quality in sufficient number to ensure the development of research and the conservation of the African archaeological heritage.

Regional and international co-operation has an essential role to play in achieving these aims, especially as archaeological research is costly and high-quality laboratory equipment is rare in Africa. For all these reasons the Béninois Archaeological Research Team supports the conclusions and recommendations on training in archaeology set out by the participants of the fifth colloquium of the West African Archaeological Association in Ouagadougou in July 1992:

Alexis B. A. Adandé

Figure 6.4 Fragment of silicified wood from the Central Sahara area
(*Photo: Musée ethnographique Alexandre Sénou Adandé*)

Figure 6.5 Part of the showcase of late prehistoric artefacts from sites at Cocotomey and Houngbanou, Benin
(*Photo: Musée ethnographique Alexandre Sénou Adandé*)

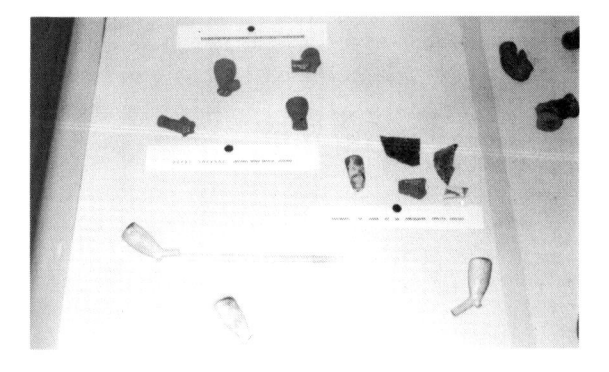

Figure 6.6 Archaeological artefacts dating from the late 17th to early 18th centuries, Allada site, Bénin
(*Photo: Musée ethnographique Alexandre Sénou Adandé*)

Figure 6.7 Archaeological artefacts from the Moru-Zakpé site, Borgu, Benin, found by a student of the Université National du Bénin
(*Photo: Musée ethnographique Alexandre Sénou Adandé*)

1. To rationalize the use of existing skills and laboratories in the region.
2. To strengthen documentary exchange networks and set up data banks.
3. To open a regional post-university archaeology training centre in the (sub-)region, the choice having judiciously fallen on the Université de Ouagadougou.

References

Adagba, C. E. 1986–87. 'Recherches archéologiques en République populaire du Bénin', *Cahiers des Archives du sol* 1, 124–53.

Adandé, A. 1992a. 'Recherche archéologique et information des publics nationaux', in *Actes des Rencontres: Quels musées pour l'Afrique? Patrimoine en devenir. Bénin, Ghana, Togo, 18–23 novembre 1991.* Paris: ICOM, pp. 227–30.

Adandé, A. 1992b. 'La question des collections archéologiques en Afrique de l'Ouest: étude de cas en République du Bénin', paper presented at the colloquium on 'L'objet archéologique africain et son devenir', Paris, 4–6 November 1992, UNESCO–CNRS.

Adandé, A. and Adagba, C. 1986. *Rapport sur l'enseignement de la préhistoire et de l'archéologie à l'Université nationale du Bénin (UNB), 1979–86,* FLASH, Abomey-Calavi: Département d'histoire et d'archéologie.

—— 1988. 'Dix années de recherche archéologiques au Bénin (1978–88)', *Nyame Akuma* 30, 3–8.

Adandé, A. and Zévounou, I. 1990. 'Education et ressources patrimoniales: expériences novatrices dans le contexte scolaire béninois', *PACT.*

—— 1994. 'Education and heritage: an example of new work in schools in Benin', in Peter G. Stone and Brian L. Molyneaux (eds). *The Presented Past, Heritage, Museums and Education. One World Archaeology,* vol. 20, pp. 315–25. London and New York: Routledge in association with English Heritage.

Souza-Ayari, R. de. 1992. 'Musées et publics scolaires: l'expérience du Musée de Porto-Novo', in *Actes et Rencontres: Quels musées pour l'Afrique? Le patrimoine en devenir, Bénin, Ghana, Togo, 18–23 novembre 1991,* Paris: ICOM, pp. 353–8.

West African Archaeological Association. 1992. *Final Document, Fifth Colloquium and General Meeting (Ougadougou, 27 July–1 August 1992).*

PART II

Museums & the Management of the Archaeological Heritage

7 Côte d'Ivoire
When Scholars Abandon the People

FOFANA LEMASSOU
Université Nationale de Côte D'Ivoire, Abidjan

This chapter was born of frustration. Since 1982, when the first agreement, since abrogated, between the Institut d'histoire, d'art et d'archéologie africains and the Directorate of the Cultural Heritage was concluded no sustained collaboration has been possible between the two institutions responsible for the management of the cultural heritage in Côte d'Ivoire. An old dispute emerged from this aborted project, which has made Ivoirien archaeologists and museum people deeply suspicious of one another. We have thus reached a situation where it is the West African Museums Programme, an institution quite foreign to Côte d'Ivoire, that is getting the two institutions to collaborate. Even then, foreign help has not prevented us from giving free rein to our disputes.

In fact one has the impression that instead of managing their cultural heritage, Ivoirien archaeologists and museum technicians are managing their personal disputes. They do not ask themselves questions about the problematic of their cultural heritage. They have a rather vague approach to their respective roles and the way they deal with heritage matters is naturally affected by it. The aim of this chapter is to raise the contradictions inherent in heritage management in Côte d'Ivoire, to set out the problematic of such management and to see how better collaboration can be achieved.

Our discussion focuses on three major points: (1) theoretical aspects, (2) contradictions in heritage management, (3) prospects.

Theoretical aspects

The definitions and theories advanced by experts on the heritage issue are many and varied.[1] Of all such approaches we prefer that of the team led by Professor Bruno Philippe of the Université de Paris IV on the preservation and enhancement of the heritage and the environment. We feel that the way those researchers see the heritage is particularly enriching for African countries, where the heritage is not yet free of suppositions and preconceptions. According to Philippe and his colleagues, the heritage needs to be defined in the context of the social order or social relations: 'the heritage is what one society accepts or rejects from another in building itself'.[2] It is thus a legacy and as such the heritage implies a testator and heirs in the legal sense of the word. It is a supremely political matter in the sense that it involves a choice to be made by the heirs (here, the people) of what their testators bequeath to them. The choice is influenced by the financial, political, affective and other concerns to which social groups are subjected when the 'choice' is made.

This helps us understand the full complexity of the heritage question, which rests on one essential notion: the bond implied by the relations that men establish with other men through a legacy. In the heritage choice, the bond takes no account of the intrinsic value of the inheritance; what is at stake is the subjective value that is attributed to it and which constructs the identity of the heirs.

Thus it will be seen that the heritage is acceptance or rejection operated in the function of a bond. The management which results necessarily reflects that bond. It will be republican in a republic, monarchical in a monarchy, theocratic in a theocracy. In the north of Côte d'Ivoire the sacred woods regarded as part of their heritage by the people are managed by animist religious authorities while the mosques are managed by imams or in a subordinate capacity by so-called Muslim families. It would never enter the head of an imam to manage a sacred wood, since he has established no bond with it. One may well wonder whether today the bond is basic in our approach to the heritage in the specific case of Côte d'Ivoire.

Incoherent heritage management

In post-colonial Côte d'Ivoire the heritage question has been hi-jacked from its social and political character and turned into a scientific problem. To bring out the point we shall analyse law No. 87-806 of 28 July 1987 on the protection of the heritage[3] and the practice regarding the heritage that has resulted from it.

Article I (chapter I) of the law defines the heritage satisfactorily, since it introduces the key notion of inheritance: 'The national cultural heritage is all the immovable and movable artefacts, folk arts and traditions, artistic, social, religious, technological and scientific styles, forms, disciplines and usages inherited from the past'. Apart from this article, reference to the heritage disappears from the text. Only the scientific criterion is taken on board. Nowhere in the other sixty-four articles of the law is there any mention of heritage or inheritors. Thus any object 'of interest from the viewpoint of history, art, science or ethnology' is regarded as part of the heritage.

There follows a specious approach to the task entrusted to museums. In article 46 (chapter IV, section I) it is stated: 'In order to preserve and illustrate the cultural heritage, notably *objets d'art*, artistic, historical, ethnographic and scientific antiquities as well as the products of excavations and discoveries, several categories of museums are established . . .'. In fact the museum serves to conserve and illustrate documents regarded by scholarship as part of the heritage. But it is not the role of scholarship to define the heritage. That role falls to the heirs of all the people, including scholars, who cannot take the place of the whole.

Since the roles are not defined, it is scarcely surprising to observe conflicts between 'institutions responsible for the management of the heritage' in Côte d'Ivoire.

For university research institutes (with their archaeologists, art historians, etc.), heritage management falls to them as of right, given that the museums manage the scientific heritage. To resolve this tricky problem, in 1992 the Ministry of Culture set up the Centre de recherches sur les arts et la culture in order to escape 'blackmail by men of learning'. But the problem remains, since each university institute holds on to the results of its own work and especially to the remains collected during its expeditions. Thus, at the Institut d'histoire, d'art et d'archéologie, archaeological excavations have been carried out and the remains collected are stored in boxes. Only on very rare occasions do we agree, with many difficulties, to lend a few objects to the museum.

Suspicion was raised to a new pitch with the discovery of the site of Gohitafla in 1983 by local people. A first expedition was got on foot the same year and since then no expedition of any size has been organized. The institute wants the Ministry of Culture to fund the work; the Ministry asserts that it is up to the institute to include it in its programme as priority research and hence to fund it from its own resources. As for the IES, it arrogates to itself paternity of the discovery and the dissemination of information about it through the media, accusing the rest of having unfrozen and misused large sums of money.

It would be tedious to mention all the examples of this nature concerning heritage management in Côte d'Ivoire. The reality is that scholars, museum professionals and political authorities have abdicated their responsibilities. The heritage question is badly posed and the responses are incoherent. So we would suggest a more coherent approach.

What is to be done?

As was stressed above, the heritage question falls within the social order and not the logical or scientific order. But our management is rather scientific. To get back to better heritage management, we need to redefine the roles of the various partners involved. They can be grouped into two categories: the university research institutes and the museums.

The former have the task of enriching teaching programmes at the university by their work and contributing to the cultural development of Côte d'Ivoire. In that sense, they are called upon to initiate research into art and culture, identifying them, analysing them and enhancing them through scholarly publications.

Once that work has been completed, the fate reserved for the documentary sources is no longer a matter for the researcher. Other institutions must take over, whose aim is to collect the sources gathered by research institutes, conserve them in an appropriate environment and ensure that they are widely disseminated among the general public. Naturally, that role falls to museums.

Yet, in their present state, are the museums capable of living up to what is expected of them? The reply can only be in the negative, since their management is marked by amateurishness: no sense of vocation, no inventories, no dynamic permanent exhibition, conceptual shortcomings among co-ordinators, etc., are all ills from which museums in Côte d'Ivoire are suffering.

It therefore appears a matter of urgency to reorganize the museums and restore to them the essential functions of preserving, documenting and disseminating the national heritage.

Furthermore, it is essential that museum policy should be decentralized. The Ministry of Culture has realized this but too timidly. It has set up regional museums which are in fact simply replications of the Musée national in Abidjan. Thought must be given to creating a large number of local museums. As a first step there is no question of creating large museums, only small ones which might be supported by local authorities. The scientific work carried out in the various regions should make it possible to set up collections and add to them regularly. Such measures will be possible only with the introduction of rules regarding documentation. They should cover the management of collections in research institutions as well as in museums.

In the former case the conditions in which, and the length of time during which, a researcher can hold on to scientific information need to be codified. That would avoid the unfortunate experience of the Institut d'histoire, where researchers have excavated sites and left no documentation of any value at the institution that funded their research. They are thus failing to live up to one of the prime missions of research institutes: the enrichment of teaching programmes and the enhancement of Ivoirien culture.

In the latter connection, museums' rules should cover the conditions under which the remains collected by researchers are transferred to museums. Once they are in a museum, their management, the conditions of research and where necessary their temporary retention must be subject to clear, unambiguous rules.

Conclusion

This brief analysis has enabled us to deal with the incoherent management of the heritage in Côte d'Ivoire. Because there is no rational definition of the heritage question the parties concerned, researchers, museum professionals and administrative authorities, spend their time settling personal scores. Every project is doomed to failure because of the weight of inertia.

If we are all to fulfil our roles effectively, it is essential to redefine each one's key task in the management and enhancement of the cultural heritage. After their work researchers must be required to hand over their documentary collections to the museums so that the latter can conserve them and disseminate them among the people, who are their true proprietors.

Notes

1. It would be tedious to list them here, our purpose being to offer not a definition but rather a consistent approach. The following are among the journals or pamphlets that have touched on this subject: *Archéologia, Monuments historiques, ICOMOS-Nouvelles* (International Council of Monuments and Sites), *Nouvelles de l'archéologie*. Colloquia are numerous; the most enlightening is the one whose proceedings were published in 1980: *Actes du colloque international, l'histoire de l'art: accès au patrimoine*, UNESCO, World Heritage Convention, Nancy 1980.
2. P. Yves Balut, 'Du patrimoine', *RAVAGE (Revue d'archéologie moderne et d'archéologie générale)* 2 (1983), 207–37, at p. 209.
3. Law No. 87-806 of 28 July 1987 on the protection of the cultural heritage in Côte d'Ivoire.

8 Mali
The Inland Delta & the Manding Mountains

TÉRÉBA TOGOLA
Institut des Sciences Humaines, Bamako

The archaeological heritage, defined as a precious, non-renewable resource, requires appropriate protection and equitable management to the benefit of the national and international community. These notions, notably the management of the archaeological heritage, have been spreading steadily since the intensification of construction work and the rise of the environmental and ecological movement in western Europe and North America after the Second World War. Thus during the 1970s new legislation was enacted everywhere on antiquities, including the archaeological heritage and its management. Africa was affected by this wave in the mid-1980s. But, there more than elsewhere, the results of archaeological research continue to be the preserve of a small group of specialists and a small urban intellectual elite. In my view the curse of archaeology in many African countries – the deterioration or destruction of national and local archaeological heritages by illegal excavation and the illicit export of archaeological items – is a direct consequence of this inequality in the dissemination of the results of archaeological research and the lack of information among the people living close to the sites. It is high time research institutions and museums turned their attention to resolving these problems so that everyone understands the concept of the archaeological heritage and the interest and respect in which it should be held.

My aim here is to examine some basic aspects of the management of the archaeological heritage in Mali, notably the relationship among archaeology, museums and the public, from the angle of the dissemination of the results of archaeological research.

The colonial era

Before dealing with the current situation we need to recall briefly the archaeological situation during the colonial period. As is only to be expected, the wealth of the archaeological heritage of Mali did not fail to attract the attention and interest of the French. But, during this period, archaeological research, carried out almost entirely by amateur archaeologists, suffered from major shortcomings in terms of methodology, the identification of objects to collect and of course the use of the products, and deprived Mali of its history. Artefact collections were primarily surface finds or those uncovered in hasty excavations, with no stratigraphy (carried out during military or scientific expeditions), or discovered during various construction projects, and they

Figure 8.1 Toladié, one of Mali's most massive occupation mounds, over 75 ha in size stratified to a depth of over 12 m. Mostly dating to the time of the Empire of Ghana (AD 400–1200), Mali's tell sites provide a great logistical challenge to archaeologists (Photo: K. C. MacDonald)

were sent to a variety of museums in the metropole or in Dakar, after the establishment of the Institut Français d'Afrique Noire (IFAN) in 1938. Although large sums were occasionally allocated by a number of organizations in the metropole (such as the Académie des inscriptions et belles-lettres, which sponsored Desplagnes's excavations of the tumuli at El Oualadji and Kili and those of Bonnel de Mezières at Koumbi Saleh), archaeology enjoyed no official encouragement. For example, there is no mention of either archaeology or prehistory in the work published by Labouret in 1932 to help colonial administrators prepare local monographs. It goes without saying that nationals, faced with the rigours of foreign rule, were little concerned by these early archaeological efforts. They were ill informed and were quite unaware of the damage being inflicted on their archaeological heritage and of the fact that magnificent artefacts, evidence of brilliant episodes in their history, were heading for various museums overseas.

In 1951 an IFAN centre was set up in Bamako, the country's first archaeological research institution. The establishment of the centre, headed by G. Szumowski, a professional archaeologist, led to the intensification of research work on the ground and to the creation of a small museum where archaeological collections were partly preserved instead of being sent to Dakar or Paris. The number of journals also increased, although they were all still published in Dakar: *Notes africaines,* starting in 1942, and the *Bulletin de l'IFAN,* starting in 1951.

Despite this marked progress, nationals remained stuck in the same roles: whether as unconcerned spectators or uninformed labourers, they took little part in the new attempts to manage their archaeological heritage.

After 1960 archaeological research took new directions. The country provided itself with an Institut des sciences humaines (ISH) which from then on regulated and managed archaeological research. At the same time, archaeological research took on an international character: work was done by archaeologists from a variety of countries: the Netherlands, the United Kingdom, the United States, Germany, etc. This situation, common to most countries in Africa, encouraged a diversity of methods, techniques and research hypotheses.

At the same time as these developments were occurring it was recognized that well prepared and executed programmes on a series of sites, if not a whole region, were necessary to get a better understanding of the life style and material culture of peoples of the past. Thanks to these changes, whose impact began to be felt only after 1970, the number of discoveries began to rise, and included the Tellem remains in the Bandiagara escarpment (Bedaux *et al.*, 1978), the neolithic mounds at Karkarichinkat, the funerary monuments (chamber tombs) near Dogo and the Jenné region of the inland delta of the Niger. All the time Malian archaeology was acquiring fundamental knowledge about our past, filling in some of the gaps that had accumulated during the colonial period.

In addition to the institutional research structure represented by the ISH, the Musée national acquired new premises in 1982, becoming distinctly more modern, better equipped and having more space in terms of exhibition halls and conservation facilities. A section of the second exhibition hall is

Current trends in Malian archaeology

Figure 8.2 Terracotta figure from Jenné-Jeno
(*Photo: Musée National du Mali*)

permanently devoted to archaeology. In addition, it puts on exhibitions or slide shows dealing with major sites or important topics in archaeology. The exhibitions 'Du Sahara au Sahel', on the prehistory of the Malian Sahara, and 'Fanfannyègèné', on a rock shelter occupied in neolithic times, organized in 1985 and 1991 respectively, belong in this framework.

But the reverse of this coin is the total absence of research structures and regional museums. Such complete concentration limits access to the archaeological programmes launched by the ISH and the Musée national to the population of Bamako alone, depriving the majority of Malians of the results of archaeological research.

Figure 8.3 Terracotta figure from Jenné-Jeno (*Photo: Musée National du Mali*)

*The Inland Delta
& the Manding Mountains*

Figure 8.4 Dr Téréba Togola (on left) at the tell site of Akumbu, Mali, where he has been directing excavations since 1990 (*Photo: K. C. MacDonald*)

This situation is felt in the public's attitude to and interest in archaeology. In 1990, when we were doing research at Méma, near the Mauritanian border, we often had occasion to discuss our research with the local people. They were always very suspicious of our explanations of the aim of our work and did not understand why we were wasting so much money and effort to collect only pottery tiles and pieces of bone. Some villagers even went so far as to suppose that I was employed by Kevin McDonald, an American student, who was taking part in the work, and that the latter was looking for antiquities that he would later sell in the United States. This example, isolated though it may be, shows that there is a real need to communicate to the people the knowledge accumulated by archaeology of the origins and aspects of their past civilizations. As stressed above, inequality in access to the results of archaeological research and the public's negative attitude towards archaeology are among the chief causes of the destruction of archaeological resources. It has been observed that people's interest in an archaeological site increases once the historical and cultural relationship between the people and the site is established (Dembélé and Van der Waals, 1991). To illustrate the point we may look briefly at the cases of two Malian regions: Jenné and the Manding mountains, just above Bamako.

The region of Jenné

In recent decades the region of Jenné has provided fundamental information about our past. The intensive work of the McIntoshes, carried out in 1977 and 1981 on the site of Jenné-Jeno and its hinterland, proves conclusively that major innovations such as the rise of urban centres, the birth and development of complex societies and inter-regional trade were all occurring in the region. In addition to this periodization, there is no longer any doubt

Těréba Togola

Figure 8.5 The large exposure (LX) at Jenné-Jeno, 1981 excavations. Jenné-Jeno remains one of West Africa's best documented tell sites, with an occupation extending from 250 BC to AD 1400 (*after S. K. McIntosh, plate 3*)

about the autochthonous character of these innovations, attributed throughout the colonial period to an external impetus.

In addition to a series of articles in several scholarly journals and two books, the McIntoshes published the results of their work in popular magazines such as the *National Geographic* and *Géo*. Offprints of the articles, intended for the general public, were distributed to local notables and administrative authorities. But it must be acknowledged that the language in which this information on Jenné-Jeno was published limits their accessibility to the Malian public. Nevertheless, these actions, to which should be added a discussion of the results at a conference organized by a local non-governmental organization, the Amis de Djenné, led the people of Jenné to become aware of the historical importance of Jenné-Jeno. Thus the Amis de Djenné, who now regard Jenné-Jeno with enormous pride, are undertaking, in collaboration with the Division of the Cultural Heritage of Mali, action to protect the site from the illegal excavations which are ravaging the whole region of the inland delta of the Niger, where the sites, which supply a large number of terracotta statues, are among the most looted in Mali and perhaps in the whole of West Africa. However, in the view of several archaeologists, perhaps as a result of the attempts at protection of the Amis de Djenné, illegal excavations, which fuel a flourishing trade in terracotta statues to western Europe and North America, have simply been driven away from Jenné-Jeno towards sites inside the Delta.

The Manding mountains

The second case relates to the classified forest of the Manding mountains. A project aimed at securing the active participation of the local people in managing natural and cultural resources (including the archaeological

Figure 8.6 A jar inhumation from the 1981 excavations at Jenné-Jeno (*Thurstan Shaw Collection, University College, London*)

heritage) is in the process of being initiated by the Opération aménagement et production forestière (OAPF), in association with the ISH. A picture illustrating various aspects of daily life at Kourounkorokalé (a rock shelter occupied in neolithic times) and the publication of articles about the same site in the Bamanan national language have already been embarked on to this end. There has been an encouraging response to these attempts, notably to

Figure 8.7 The Haute Vallée at the frontier of Mali and Guinea. It was from this area in the Manding mountains that the Mali Empire developed (*Photo: K. C. MacDonald*)

the picture, designed to alert the village people to the historic and cultural importance of archaeological sites. We have been asked for copies of the picture in several villages in the Manding mountains. In addition, the existence of other sites in the region (some, from what the villagers say, still have a cultural significance) has been pointed out to us.

The cases of Jenné and the Manding mountains cannot be concluded without mention of the debate on the publication and dissemination of the results of archaeological research. These have often been regarded as representing a threat to the objects and sites from which the objects come. But surely the best way of protecting the objects dug up during excavations is publishing them. In the event of a dispute the country of origin can then prove ownership and thus facilitate their repatriation. Moreover, in the case of the Jenné region and the whole inland delta, where many archaeological sites are threatened with destruction, are not the scientific excavations whose results are properly published themselves acts of conservation?

Conclusion

These cases show that there is an urgent need to communicate the results of archaeological research to the public. All our efforts to protect the archaeological heritage will be doomed to failure if the majority of nationals (notably the communities living near sites) do not understand and do not share this concern. To remedy the present situation the establishment of proper regional out-stations of the ISH and regional museums, all run by committed individuals (archaeologists, museologists or local volunteers), must be planned. The establishment of museums near major archaeological sites such as Jenné-Jeno must also be contemplated. Such museums, where some of the objects found during archaeological excavations on those sites would

Figure 8.8 The rockshelter site of Korounkorokalé, Mali under excavation in 1993. The site features Mali's longest occupation ranging from the early Holocene to the present day. The excavators are the author and K. MacDonald (*Photo: K. C. MacDonald*)

be deposited, must be run by museologists or archaeologists, but with the active participation of the local people, so that the latter do not feel left out. These new structures must adopt educational programmes – visits to the site and to on-going archaeological excavations; slide and documentary film shows; if possible, small travelling exhibitions – aimed at schools and the public.

References

Bedaux, R., Constandse-Westermann, T. S., Hacquebord, L., Lange, A. G. and Van der Waals, J. D. 1978. 'Recherches archéologiques dans le Delta intérieur du Niger', *Paleohistoria* 20, 92–220.

Dembélé, M. and Van der Waals, J. D. 1991. 'Looting the antiquities of Mali', *Antiquity* 65 (249), 904–5.

Holl, A. 1990. 'West African archaeology: colonialism and nationalism', in Peter Robertshaw (ed.), *The History of African Archaeology*, London: James Currey.

Labouret, H. 1932. 'Plan de monographie régionale', *Bulletin du Comité d'études historiques et scientifiques d'AOF* 15, 549–91.

Liesegang, G. 1975. 'Results of the excavations at Famambougou, Mali', *Nyame Akuma*, 27–8.

McIntosh, S. K. and McIntosh, R. J. 1980. *Prehistoric Investigations in the Region of Jenne, Mali*. Cambridge Monographs in African Archaeology 2, Oxford: BAR.

Obayemi, H. 1969. 'History of Archaeology in West Africa'. M.A. dissertation, University of Legon, Ghana.

Raimbault, M. 1981. 'Les recherches archéologiques du Mali: histoire, bilan, problèmes et perspectives', *Recherche, pédagogie et culture* 55, 16–25.

Smith, A. 1974. 'Preliminary report on excavations at Karkarichinkat-sud, Tilemsi valley, Republic of Mali', *West African Journal of Archaeology* 4, 33–55.

9 Nigeria
The Case of Jos Museum

ANTHONIA K. FATUNSIN
National Commission for Museums and Monuments, Ibadan

This chapter looks into what the archaeological heritage means in the Nigerian context, and what the policy of the Nigerian government, through its agency, the National Commission for Museums and Monuments, is towards the protection and management of archaeological resources. Jos Museum will be used as a case study to show how the National Commission for Museums and Monuments has achieved this objective. The chapter also highlights the problems faced by the Commission in the discharge of its responsibilities and makes some recommendations.

At this stage, it becomes necessary to provide working definitions of the terms 'archaeology', 'the heritage' and 'management'. Archaeology is a science concerned with the reconstruction of ancient ways of life from material remains. It is a search for knowledge about the past of a people for the purpose of rediscovering and understanding their existence better. The heritage is a legacy: it is what we inherit from others; it is what is bequeathed to us. The fact that it was inherited makes it dear to us, makes us want to treasure it and guard it well so that we can derive maximum benefit from it. The heritage is a tool that is basic to the existence of a people in all walks of life (Naqvri, 1980). It should be regarded as a real local resource base on which to build a strong and viable future (Andah, 1990). For our purpose, management means controlling, directing, organizing and looking after. The management of the archaeological heritage therefore means protecting it and administering it in its original environment and in its relationship to history and contemporary society (Bjornstad, 1989).

Among the major functions of a museum are the collection, storage and preservation of items of material culture from both the past and the present. The objects, if not well preserved and properly managed, may not serve the purposes which they are meant to serve – educational and recreational, leading to an awareness on the part of the community or the populace of their rich cultural past for the purpose of guiding them towards a more meaningful future.

Archaeological heritage

The International Committee on the Management of the Archaeological Heritage (ICMAH) has defined the archaeological heritage as 'that part of the material heritage for which archaeological methods provide primary information. It comprises all vestiges of human existence and consists of

Figure 9.1 The Jos Museum, founded in 1952

places relating to all vestiges of human activity, together with all the *portable* cultural material associated with them'. (ICMAH, Charter for the Protection and Management of the Archaeological Heritage, 1989). It is a major, endangered and non-renewable resource needed by the people for their history (McIntosh, 1992).

In the Nigerian context the archaeological heritage, according to federal government decree No. 77 of 1979, comprises fossil remains of man, or of animals found in association with man, the ruins of abandoned settlements, middens, sacred places, caves and natural shelters, any engraving, drawing, inscription or painting on rock, any stone object or implement believed to have been fashioned or used by early man, any fortification, wall, earthwork, bridge, shrine, excavation, monolith or grave, any ancient tool, of metal, wood or clay, textiles, or leather, which is of archaeological interest. It also includes any land on which archaeological materials are thought likely to be discovered.

National Commission for Museums and Monuments policies

No nation can preserve and manage its heritage effectively without enacting appropriate laws. The first set of laws in this direction is contained in the Antiquities Ordinance of 1953, which came into force ten years after the establishment of the Nigerian Antiquities Service (later the Federal Department of Antiquities). The ordinance charged the Antiquities Commission with responsibility for guiding and protecting archaeological research in the country. Anybody wishing to conduct an archaeological excavation must obtain permission from the commission. The ordinance states, 'No person shall by means of excavation or similar operations search for any antiquities unless authorized by permit, issued by the commission and with the consent of the State Government in whose territory the search is to be carried out'. At another point it states that 'The commission shall, before issuing a permit under the section, satisfy itself that the applicant is competent by training and experience to carry out the operations for which the permit was required and may, at its discretion, require to be satisfied that the person has the financial means to do so.' The ordinance protects archaeological sites from being plundered and stipulates that no amateur or non-professional may carry out any excavation. The ordinance gave the local authority of the area where a discovery has been made the power to take custody of the find or keep it in an approved museum.

In 1974 the Antiquities (Prohibited Transfer) Decree No. 9 was promulgated. This decree affected all objects regarded as antiquities, including objects of archaeological significance. Its promulgation was informed by the alarming rate at which Nigerian art objects were disappearing, smuggled across the border to meet the increasing demand for Nigerian art pieces overseas. The decree provided for the protection of antiquities and vested their purchase in the Federal Department of Antiquities. Only the department could buy antiquities. Decree No. 9 laid down stiff penalties, ranging from fines to imprisonment, for contravention of its terms. Anyone convicted forfeits the objects to the federal government. Anybody wishing to export antiquities is required to obtain a permit from the controlling agency and anybody who wilfully damages any antiquity for which a permit has been refused could also be penalized.

Decree No. 77 of 1979 dissolved the Federal Department of Antiquities, replacing it with the National Commission for Museums and Monuments. This new body was given wider powers. By the terms of the decree it is the only body authorized by law to organize excavations without first seeking permission from a government agency, save only, that it must, as a matter of courtesy, consult traditional rulers and local government heads of areas to be excavated. Chance discoveries must be reported to the commission within seven days or the discoverer faces litigation. The commission's agent has the right to suspend any excavation indefinitely until the commission is satisfied. The decree provides for the imposition of a 500,000 naira fine or six months' imprisonment or both on anyone convicted of contravening this section of the decree. The power of the local authority to retain discovered items was removed under this decree.

Experience, however, shows that, though permits were applied for and granted to professionals, the issuing body seldom received information about the results of the excavation or research, with the result that only the number of permits granted was known. There were neither reports nor publications to back them up. Some expatriates even departed with their field notes and the excavated materials. Effective control was lacking. To improve matters, in 1988 excavation permit forms (both application and permit) were designed for expatriate and indigenous archaeologists. Before then the permit took the form of an ordinary letter.

The permit for expatriates stipulates that all excavated material must remain in the country of origin and must be deposited with the museum nearest to the excavation site or with the institution to which the researcher is affiliated. Datable materials which need analysis, for which the facilities are not available in the country, are allowed to be taken out so long as they are returned after analysis. The permit also states that copies of field notes, sketches, drawings, maps and photographs should be deposited with the National Commission. As regards indigenous archaeologists, reports should be forwarded within the stipulated period and copies of publications should be made available to the commission. Though not stipulated on the permit, it is a condition that a senior archaeologist from the commission should participate in the research activities of expatriate archaeologists.

The result has been encouraging. The forms came into use in 1990 and resulted in an influx of material and reports into the research department of the Commission.

Exchange

Archaeological materials are exchanged by the commission within its establishment only. Allowance is also made for archaeological artefacts to be sent out on loan for a period of time. When Nigerian antiquities travel for exhibition abroad a keeper from the commission accompanies them for security purposes and ensures the safe return of the objects.

As part of the effort to involve the state governments in the management of the cultural heritage, in 1988 the states' Councils for Arts and Culture were advised to see the preservation of the country's cultural heritage as the responsibility not of the federal government alone but as theirs too. They were encouraged to set up their own museums, declare their own monuments and employ their own cultural resource personnel, such as archaeologists, enthographers, curators, conservators and superintendents of monuments.

The very first group of museums to be established could be referred to as site museums, since they are located in places where archaeological discoveries have been made or in their immediate vicinity. They are Esie Museum in Kwara State, Ife Museum in Osun State and Jos Museum in Plateau State.

Jos Museum

Jos, popularly known as the 'Tin City' since the discovery of tin deposits there, is in the north of Nigeria and is the capital of Plateau State. The collection of objects dug up during tin-mining operations in the 1920s and 1930s attracted the attention of archaeologists. The very first discovery, the terracotta head of a monkey, was washed out of the tin-bearing gravel in 1928 and was taken to the embryonic museum of the Department of Mines in Jos. More articles continued to turn up. In 1944 B. E. B. Fagg visited the tin mines and observed that a lot of archaeological material was being lost during the operations. He solicited the co-operation of the miners, asking them to report their finds to him. Fagg was later appointed a government archaeologist. Consequent upon the discoveries, Jos Museum was founded to house the archaeological materials that were found in alluvial deposits during tin mining. It was also to serve as an archaeological research museum.

Initially the materials were stored in an isolated corn store in open farmland on the outskirts of Jos. Later Fagg rented a house at Bukuru, some miles away. It was not until 1952 that a multi-purpose museum was built. At the time it was opened the museum had a gallery, store, library, workroom, laboratory, darkroom, garages and offices, which were to facilitate the research activities of the Antiquities Service.

At its inception the museum aroused great public interest, especially among the miners, who were enthused to see the materials recovered by them on exhibition and at the same time encouraged to bring in more items. Jos Museum soon became the headquarters of the Federal Department of Antiquities and remained so for many years until it was transferred to Lagos. In time the museum grew into a complex of museums, consisting of the Pottery Museum, which exhibits pots from all over the country, the Tin Museum, which depicts vividly the technology of tin mining, and the Museum of Traditional Nigerian Architecture, which has reproductions of traditional architecture from all over the country. The Jos Museum also has a zoological garden.

Research

The fact that Bernard Fagg was an archaeologist actually influenced the orientation of work in the museum. A lot of effort was concentrated on archaeological research. After the initial discoveries in the Nok valley, Fagg observed that the finds continued to grow in number. He therefore created an archaeological reserve of 4 ha in the Nok valley for future research (Jemkur, 1992). From his time until the Departments of Archaeology and archaeology units were established in Nigerian universities, Jos Museum, as the headquarters of the Federal Department of Antiquities, was solely responsible for the organization of archaeological research, and the museum became the headquarters of the archaeology division of the department. The research undertaken by archaeologists in the division is twofold: (1) reconnaissance and excavation, (2) the study of material already in the stores. In 1973 archaeologists in the division excavated a late Stone Age site at Dutsen Kongba, some 13 km from Jos.

Between 1972 and 1975 more than 3,000 stone axes in the archaeology store were studied. The period 1977–82 witnessed intensive archaeological reconnaissance activity in Nigeria's newly designated Federal Capital Territory, Abuja. The commission also engages in joint archaeological projects with the archaeology departments of the University of Ibadan and the University of Nigeria, Nsukka, at Tse Dura in Benue State and Ugwelle Uturu in Abia State. But since 1987 research activity has dwindled, owing to the financial situation in the country. The division has therefore been engaged in commissioned work for Councils for Arts and Culture and tourism organizations, identifying archaeological sites and other cultural resources that could be developed for tourism. The division also participates in projects conducted by expatriates. In 1992, at a workshop organized for researchers in the commission, a three-year programme for archaeological reconnaissance and site documentation was drawn up. Its implementation was to begin in 1993 with five states. The aim is to produce an archaeological map of the country. This project has yet to take off, because of lack of funds.

Figure 9.2 Nok Terracotta, Old Kafanchan (*Photo: Jos Museum*)

Archaeological collection

Jos Museum is the only museum in Nigeria that has a separate store for archaeological artefacts. It houses all the material that has come into the museum since Fagg's day and about 80 per cent of all archaeological materials recovered by the staff of the commission are preserved there. It is divided in two – the Nok Room, where only materials from the Nok culture are kept, and the general store. The material in the store is documented and kept in wooden boxes, which are arranged serially on Dexion racks. There is also a catalogue, which contains information about the material in the store. The catalogue serves as a guide to any researcher who may want to retrieve artefacts from the store for study. The Jos Museum archaeological collection renders research facilities available to scholars, especially those studying the Stone Age and the Nok culture. Artefacts are also loaned by the museum for educational programmes in institutions and for exhibition, while students of archaeology are brought to the division for enlightenment.

Communication

The museum communicates with the public through displays, lectures/seminars and publications.

Education

A Centre for Training Museum Technicians was established in 1963 by UNESCO. Then it served as a bilingual regional centre for Africa south of the Sahara. It is now being administered by the National Commission for Museums and Monuments. The Institute of Archaeology and Museum Studies came into being in 1989 and five years later the Centre for Preventative Conservation in Tropical Africa (PREMA) took off. The motive behind the establishment of these schools was to provide adequate skill in the proper care not only of archaeological resources but also of other aspects of the cultural heritage, including monuments. The museum has also an education unit which is responsible for conducting outreach programmes.

Today Jos Museum is a major attraction, not only to the people of the locality and the country at large but also to expatriates living in or visiting Nigeria. The museum complex is much patronized on festive occasions by every segment of society, rich or poor, young or old.

Appraisal

Although a basis has been established for the management of the country's archaeological heritage by the National Commission for Museums and Monuments, a lot still has to be done to raise the standard. The following points need looking into.

1. At the inception of Jos Museum the material first exhibited was that discovered by tin miners, who knew little or nothing about archaeology. The organization of archaeological research in Nigeria does not take cognizance of amateurs; only experienced archaeologists have been addressed. It is my view that the interest of amateurs in prehistoric research should be enlisted. Amateurs could assist in archaeological surveys and excavations. In so doing their interest in archaeology will develop and possibly with time they could become professionals.

2. Jos Museum recorded a heavy turn-out of visitors within the first few months of its establishment because the objects that made up the display came from the locality and the people were interested in what was being discovered around them. The museum was a source of pride. It aroused their enthusiasm and increased awareness of their cultural past. Apart from a few local museums, most museums in Nigeria are situated in state capitals or in urban centres far from the places of discovery, with the result that only the enlightened and the rich can visit them. There is a need to create small museums near places of archaeological interest or in local government areas. Such a step would increase awareness among local people of their past. It would help them appreciate the value of their heritage and encourage them to discover and report finds in their locality. In 1979 the establishment of museums ceased to be the exclusive right of the commission. Private museums can now be established with the approval of the commission. The power of local governments to retain excavated material which was withdrawn by Decree 77 of 1979 should be reinstated and the commission should encourage the exhibition of such material in small museums. Proliferation of museums is one of the surest ways of generating interest in the material heritage of the African people.

3. Documentation of archaeological collections follows the old system. The only record of articles in the archaeology store is the register (catalogue). In 1990 a sudden downpour in Jos flooded the archaeology store. The catalogue was badly defaced and had to be dried in the sun before what was written in it was legible again. It is therefore necessary to explore other systems. Computerized systems of documentation should be adopted. They would be less time-consuming, information would be stored permanently and searches could be conducted without difficulty.

4. Video documentation of archaeological excavations should also be encouraged. This is very effective when it comes to presentation. Video-recording captures visitors' attention and makes them appreciate and understand the exhibition better than when they merely see the objects. Such tapes could be dubbed for other organizations that may require them or they could be stored for future use.

5. Proper management requires a systematic approach to archaeological research, and adequate funding. Both are lacking. At a workshop organized for researchers at the commission in 1992 I stressed that archaeological work is still conducted haphazardly, with each archaeologist submitting a proposal to work near to or in his own area. Proposals change with staff transfers; the old proposal is abandoned and a fresh one submitted. This has led to disjointed efforts and lack of co-ordination. The financial situation of the commission has not helped, either. The result is that our archaeologists participate in projects over which they have little or no control – in most cases the projects are controlled by expatriates.

Government should pay attention to culture and give adequate financial backing to its study, since the 'cultural heritage constitutes the core of a society's cultural identity' (Jaycox, 1992).

Adequate supervision is lacking for postgraduate students carrying out their field projects. Our institutions are guilty of this. Experienced

Figure 9.3 Nok terracotta head, Katsina-Ala (*Photo: Jos Museum*)

Figure 9.4 Rop rock shelter: materials and artefacts from here are in the Jos Museum archaeology store

professionals/lecturers are issued with excavation permits to enable them to supervise the projects of their students. But what do we see? Either the lecturer abandons the student or the student, without the knowledge of the lecturer, sneaks out and conducts his excavation without supervision. Damage has been done to archaeological sites in this way. Again, once a permit has been given our institutions often ignore the issuing agent and barely communicate again until another permit is needed. Reports are not sent in or projects are not made available. The commission should be seen to enforce the obligation on the applicant as regards supervision and the submission of reports and publications. By so doing the controlling agency would have an accurate record of excavated sites together with information about them. The results of research should be made public in good time and in a language which lay people can understand. Hitherto our language has been very technical and cannot be understood by non-professionals.

The most pertinent of the problems is the increasing rate of destruction of archaeological sites by public bodies or private firms during large-scale construction. The problem is not peculiar to Nigeria but affects most developing countries. The Archaeological Association of Nigeria has been unequivocal in its demand for government to legislate against any developmental construction involving earth movement without the presence of archaeologists. The government should learn a lesson from advanced countries, where archaeological rescue operations are built into construction contracts. Archaeologists should be the first on the scene at construction sites for prospecting purposes and should be present throughout for salvage operations. Only in this way can we ensure that the archaeological heritage is not destroyed.

References

Andah, B. W. 1990. Prologue to 'Cultural resource management: an African dimension', in B. W. Andah (ed.), *Cultural Resource Management.* Ibadan: Wisdom Publishers.

Antiquities Service. 1948. *Annual Report.*

Bjornstad, M. 1989. 'The ICOMOS International Committee on Archaeological Heritage Management', in H. Cleere (ed.), *Archaeological Heritage Management in the Modern World.* London: Unwin Hyman.

Colony and Protectorate of Nigeria. 1953. An Ordinance to provide for the Preservation of Antiquities and for Purposes connected therewith.

Federal Department of Antiquities. 1978. *Twenty-five years of Jos Museum.* Jos: National Museums.

Federal Government of Nigeria. 1974. Antiquities (Prohibited Transfers) Decree.

—— 1979. Decree No. 77 establishing the National Commission for Museums and Monuments.

Jaycox, E. V. K. 1992. Opening remarks of the Vice-president, African Region, the World Bank, at the International Conference on Culture and Development in Africa. Washington, D.C.: International Bank for Reconstruction and Development.

Jemkur, J. F. 1992. *Aspects of the Nok Culture.* Zaria: Ahmadu Bello University Press.

McIntosh, S. 1992. 'Archaeological Heritage Management and Site Inventory Systems in Africa'. Paper presented at the International Conference on Culture and Development in Africa, Washington, D.C.

Mare, A. O. 1992. 'Community Participation in the Conservation of Cultural Heritage'. Paper presented at the International Conference on Culture and Development in Africa, Washington, D.C.

Naqvri, S. 1980. Address by the Representative of the Director General of UNESCO, in *Proceedings of the Twelfth and Thirteenth General Assembly of the International Council of Museums.*

National Commission for Museums and Monuments. 1983. *A Source Book for Nigerian Archaeology.* Jos: National Commission for Museums and Monuments.

10 Burkina Faso
Museums & the Archaeological Heritage

ANTOINE MILLOGO KALO

Université de Ouagadougou

Museums and Archaeology

One has to go back to the colonial period to understand the history and current organization of museums and archaeological research in Burkina Faso.

Museums and archaeology in Burkina Faso originated in the Institut Français d'Afrique Noire (IFAN), set up in Dakar in 1938. In 1950 an outstation of IFAN opened in Ouagadougou. It began work in 1954. This centre was staffed mainly by expatriate researchers, chiefly French, with some Voltaics in a subordinate capacity (guides, interpreters). It was in the framework of the research activities of these European researchers that ethnographic objects were collected and archaeological remains discovered. Within the IFAN Ouagadougou centre a museum section was set up informally where ethnographic objects and archaeological remains were kept. This section was the embryo of the future Musée national in Ouagadougou.

In 1960, at independence, IFAN in Ouagadougou became the Centre Voltaïque de la Recherche Scientifique (CVRS). The museum remained there with no links with archaeological research.

In 1962 the National Assembly of Upper Volta created the Musée national in Ouagadougou, attached to the Office of the President. As for archaeology, there were no national researchers trained in that discipline and no research programme existed. Given the quantity of remains amassed and piled up in the museum, this institution ought to have promoted archaeological research.

The life of the museum right down to the present day has been marked by repeated changes of supervising body (Office of the President, Ministry of National Education, Ministry of Youth and Sports, Ministry of Information and Culture) and frequent changes of premises (CVRS and CNRST, Cours normal des jeunes filles, Prytanée Militaire, private house, refectory of the Lycée Bogodogo). No research is done at the museum for lack of trained personnel.

Archaeological research in Burkina started at the Université de Ouagadougou. In 1972 Jean-Baptiste Kiéthéga gave the first lectures in archaeology there. In 1976 the archaeology laboratory opened with a research project on metals, including one on traditional techniques of exploiting gold (see Kiéthéga, 1983) and another on traditional ironworking

Antoine Millogo Kalo

Figure 10.1 Iron-ore mine shaft, Youba, Burkina Faso (*Photo: Alexis Adandé*)

techniques (project continuing). This work helped promote archaeology in Burkina Faso and also helped train Burkinabe archaeologists.

It can be seen that the museum and archaeology have evolved along parallel lines, giving rise to the present situation.

The current situation

There are no institutional links between museums and archaeology in Burkina Faso. The two fields come under different supervising Ministries. Museums come under the Ministry of Culture, archaeology under the Ministry of Secondary and Higher Education and Scientific Research. This institutional parallelism seems to be a step backwards, compared with the situation during the colonial period. The Musée national and the provincial museums exist without archaeological research, and in these locations without exhibition halls archaeologists pile up remains collected from excavations. The ideal would be to establish a link between the museums and archaeology, with archaeology providing the remains and the museums exhibiting them to the public.

Joint action has been tried in the area of exhibiting the results of archaeological research.

In 1989 an exhibition of the Club d'histoire Cheikh Anta Diop (a student history club) presented archaeological remains from Burkina at the Maison de la Presse Mohamed Maïga.

In 1991 the same club exhibited some archaeological remains in connection with tourism on the premises of the Musée national.

In 1990, on the occasion of ICOMOS day, an exhibition on housing in Burkina Faso presented archaeological remains at the Georges Melliès French Cultural Centre. The exhibition was organized jointly by the archaeology laboratory of the Université de Ouagadougou and the Directorate of the Cultural Heritage, under which the museums come.

In 1990 an exhibition of the Museum Department displayed funerary vases found in archaeological excavations.

After the Abidjan meeting the 'Vallées du Niger' exhibition initiated by the Musée national des arts africains et océaniens in Paris showed archaeological remains and objects from the collections of the Musée national.

Thus attempts are being made to bring the museums and archaeology closer together. But much remains to be done. To succeed, several types of action are required:

1. Establishing institutional links between museums and archaeological research.

2. Recruiting archaeologists to the museum who can carry out archaeological research there.

3. Equipping the present museum with adequate premises so as to enable it to mount exhibitions showing the results of excavation. The Ministry of Culture's proposal to build a national museum will help to overcome this handicap.

Figure 10.2a (*left*) The large furnace at Youba (*Photo: Alexis Adandé*)

Figure 10.2b (*right*) Close-up of the large furnace at Youba (*Photo: Alexis Adandé*)

The rules governing archaeological research come under two different Ministries. Research permits are issued by the Centre national de la recherche scientifique et technique (CNRST, formerly IFAN), after taking the advice of the archaeology laboratory of the Université de Ouagadougou. The CNRST and the archaeology laboratory come under the Ministry of Secondary and Higher Education and Scientific Research. The management,

Legislation on research and the management of the archaeological heritage

conservation and preservation of collections and sites come under the Directorate of Cultural Heritage within the Ministry of Culture.

This situation, with two bodies supervising research and the protection of the archaeological heritage, creates a conflict of responsibility and renders management of the heritage ineffective. Only the research aspects (methods and techniques of excavation, analyses and publications) have prevailed in the realm of archaeology. The archaeology laboratory of the Université de Ouagadougou, which carries out the bulk of archaeological research, does not have the material, financial or human means to protect the archaeological heritage. As for the Directorate of the Cultural Heritage, responsible for its management, preservation and protection, it has no archaeologists assigned to the task. It would seem difficult for a department to manage something about whose scientific features it knows nothing.

Prospects of solutions

The current situation of museums and archaeology creates a double feeling of frustration. On the one hand, archaeologists are frustrated at seeing the results of their work confined solely to the scientific and academic aspects for lack of exhibitions to inform the broader public. On the other, the activity of museums remains essentially ethnographic (collections, conservation) for lack of archaeological work that would make it possible to give a historical dimension to exhibitions.

The alternative lies, in reality, at the human level, notably in the training of museologists,. We feel it is easier to train an archaeologist in museology than to attempt the reverse. It is therefore imperative in the recruitment of museologists to give priority to applicants who have had practical training in archaeology on the ground.

Reference

Kiéthiéga, Jean-Baptiste. 1983. *L'Or de la Volta noire.* Paris: Karthala.

11 Senegal
Towards a New Policy to Protect Sites and Monuments

ABDOULAYE CAMARA
Musée Historique, Gorée

The National Heritage Directorate was set up in 1967. It comes under the Ministry of Culture, and in addition to bearing responsibility for protecting cultural assets, it is responsible for issuing permits for archaeological excavations and exercising permanent supervision over the national heritage.

Since the independence of Senegal two legal instruments have governed heritage protection policy: law No. 71–12 of 25 January 1971, containing provisions relating to historic monuments and excavations and discoveries, and decree No. 73-746 of 8 August 1973, bringing it into force. The legislation is organized under five main heads:

1. Immovable objects.
2. Movable objects, with, in particular, classification of movable objects belonging to the state, those belonging to a local authority or an institution, and those belonging to individuals.
3. Protecting and preserving historic monuments.
4. Excavations and finds.
5. The Commission supérieure des monuments historiques.

The necessary regulations thus exist. But a law without arrangements to make it effective remains a dead letter.

Since these regulations were adopted many discoveries have been made, and methods of conducting archaeological excavations and protecting archaeological remains have evolved, without Senegalese legislation following the shift.

A Commission supérieure des monuments historiques functioned for a few years after it was established before disappearing into oblivion. But the job of the commission, whose secretariat was provided by the Directorate of the Historic and Ethnographic Heritage, was to discuss all problems relating to excavations and establish a dialogue between teams of researchers and the public services.

A preliminary list of classified sites was drawn up in 1970.[1] Subsequently it was amended to conform with the provisions of law No. 71-12 of 25 January 1971.[2] These two ministerial orders emanated from the Directorate of the Historic and Ethnographic Heritage of the Ministry of Culture.

Outside prehistoric and protohistoric sites, some 100 sites are classified. Of these, 40 per cent are buildings, forts or stations built under the colonial occupation. By comparison with the problems of conservation encountered on other sites, here only a fifth of the buildings have deteriorated to a state of ruin. Their relatively good condition is explained by the fact that most such

Abdoulaye Camara

Figure 11.1 Neolithic site at Sénoudébou, Tambacounda region. Erosion of the marigots reveals the remains that are to be found in the waterways

buildings have been occupied by Ministries, governorates or prefectures. Places of worship, notably mosques and churches (20 per cent of classified sites), are being satisfactorily conserved because the people who are their direct heirs or who visit them are aware of their value. Natural or scenic sites (20 per cent) are more or less conserved according to their tourist value.

Archaeological sites are classified very vaguely, depending on the region. Because there are so many,[3] there is no hope, given the state's limited means, of implementing an effective policy to protect, safeguard and restore them.[4] The remains of Senegalese fortifications (*tata*) have completely disappeared or been reduced to heaps of loose stones sometimes marking the lines of the enclosing walls.

Wherein lies the difficulty of protecting our cultural assets, the evidence of our various traditions and achievements? While the 1971 law provides for the classification and protection of sites of historic interest, their conservation is the responsibility of the Ministry of Culture and Communication, of which the Directorate of the Cultural and Ethnographic Heritage is part. As for the historical study of them, that is the task of the Université Cheikh Anta Diop, where the Department of Prehistory and Protohistory at the Institut Fondamental d'Afrique Noire Cheikh Anta Diop (for archaeological problems) and the history departments of IFAN and the Faculty of Letters and Human Sciences are to be found. Protection of the heritage will have to rely on close co-operation among the various departments. And that is not always what obtains.

Prehistoric sites

In the current state of our knowledge, research in prehistoric archaeology makes it possible to date the appearance of the first men in Senegal to about 350,000 years ago.

Developed Old Stone Age

Sites of this cultural phase are to be found on the Petite Côte near the Tiémassass and Somone marigot, where they are pillaged by weekend tourist collectors; in the Thiès region, at Taïba, where they are ploughed up by the machines exploiting phosphates; and in the Cape Verde region, where they are threatened by the urbanization of Dakar and by market gardening.

Late Stone Age sites

Five facies have been found in Senegal.

1. North coast late Stone Age, dated to 3298-2275 BC, the Khant site of which in the Saint-Louis region has today completely disappeared as a result of quarrying for seashell material for road construction and for work on the Diama dam.

2. Cap Manuel (Dakar) or Diack (Thiès) late Stone Age. Cap Manuel, dated to 3000 BC, is today one vast dump and deathtrap despite the installation of a stairway leading to the site and an attempt to enhance its tourism potential. At Diack, despite the classification of an area inside the quarry from which basalt is extracted, the site and remains continue to be disturbed by quarrying activity.

3. The microlithic late Stone Age developed in western Senegal, notably in the dune areas, where the evidence consists of small implements (microliths) cut in silex. The sites here are exploited in the form of sandpits. The Njenawat site at Rufisque has been carried away by lorries and no longer exists. The sandpit at Diakhité, just outside Thiès, has been exploited since 1948. It is known to every collector and assistance worker living in Senegal, and for a mouthful of bread they buy beads, whole pieces of pottery, polished axes, bracelets and skulls from the quarrymen.

4. The late Stone Age in the Senegal and Ferlo valley, about which little is known. The development of irrigated areas following the construction of the dam on the Senegal river, combined with the encroachment of villages on to archaeological areas, is a threat to these sites.

5. The late Stone Age on the Falémé: the sites are situated in the silty-clayey sands of the embankment overlooking the river, or along its banks. Today they are dug out by gullies and small marigots that create vast 'badlands' in the valley.

Figure 11.2 Lump of iron-bearing sandstone showing scoring, from Thiès. Today it is a cult object, said to bear the hoofprint of the prophet Mohammed's camel

The case of the Cape Verde promontory

This region is where most economic activity is concentrated and the area of Senegal most affected by urbanization and population movement. Numerous pre- and proto-historic sites have been identified there. In 1975 the last census noted seventy-six sites of various cultures (early Stone Age, late Stone Age and Age of Metals). But the real number is likely to be much higher.

The wealth of historical remains in this region seems to be associated with the availability and good quality of the stone used in making implements: Ypres flint, chert near Sébikotane and Bargny, black flint of lutetian limestone (which provided most of the small late Stone Age tools) and volcanic dolerite in the Mamelles (virtually all the grinding material).

Prehistoric populations were settled in the Cape Verde promontory from a very early date. Evidence of early Stone Age civilizations has been found around Bargny and Sébikotane (very large middle Stone Age Mousteroid facies

Figure 11.3 Neolithic pottery from Dakar-Hann, Cape Verde: several pieces have come from sandpits in western Senegal that are used as quarries (*Photo: C. Descamps*)

industries). In the dune areas of Rufisque (Njenawat, Kounoune), late Stone Age cultures are marked by geometrically shaped microlithic tools. Along the northern Atlantic coast, notably near Lake Retba, major shell middens are evidence of protohistoric occupation. Possible solutions might be:

1. To protect and suggest classifying some areas where especially numerous or interesting remains are to be found.

2. To mark out areas in the various regions where all heritage-endangering activities should be banned.

For the effective protection of archaeological sites, four areas can be defined on the Cape Verde promontory:

1. The Deni-Youssouf ravine, where major early Stone Age and late Stone Age evidence can be found in the stratigraphy.

2. Remains on the Bargny-Est plateau on the fringes of the Bakhadiakh marigot, where strong concentrations of Mousterian-like industries have been noted.

3. The dune system north-east of the village of Kounoune, rich in late Stone Age microliths.

4. Around Lake Retba, both for the protohistoric shell deposits, unfortunately already partly exploited, and on general environmental and nature protection grounds.

Protection of prehistoric sites is often more theoretical than real. Sometimes there is no attempt to make the local people more aware of the importance of the sites. All attempts have been short-lived.

Protohistoric sites

Protohistorical remains correspond to Iron Age cultures. Four types of remains are to be found in Senegal, two of them in the form of monuments.

Figure 11.4 Neolithic site at Diakité, Thiès region. The creation of sandpits has led to the loss of many prehistoric implements, most of which have been sold to tourists or aid-workers

Figure 11.5a Excavation of a shell midden at Dionewar, Saloum islands: archaeological excavations have confirmed the artifical origin of the heaps of shells which also include pieces of pottery, household waste, burials, jewellery, etc.
(*Photo: M. Condamin*)

Shell middens are to be found all along the coast and in the estuaries of the main rivers (the Senegal, the Sine-Saloum, the Gambia and the Casamance). These sites, dating from the fourth to the fourteenth centuries AD, are made up of heaps of empty shells (arca, mangrove oyster, murex) forming artificial mounds of varying sizes. Most shell middens are today exploited as quarries. The heap at Faboura, 450 m long and 10 m high, has completely disappeared because it has been worked by the Public Works Department. It is not uncommon to see in the little port of Kaolack, and in the islands, canoes full of shells gathered on ancient sites. This sort of exploitation in the form of quarrying is all the more deplorable because the sites contain household goods, such as items of pottery, jewellery and weapons, which disappear without trace or are sold to tourists.

Measures to take:
 1. Banning and putting an end to the exploitation of some middens.
 2. Classifying the twenty-nine middens surmounted by a tumulus.
 3. Drawing the attention of customs patrols, national park officials and policemen to the situation and asking them to make regular visits.
 4. Informing the local population about the importance of conserving and safeguarding the sites.

Over 300 sites on the river Senegal are listed, corresponding to old settlement sites. They take the form of small mounds or refuse dumps made up of household waste, the remains of furnaces used in iron processing, pottery tiles, terracotta objects and burial places. The site of Sinthiou Bara (near Matam) has yielded dates from the fifth century AD to the eleventh.

Shell middens

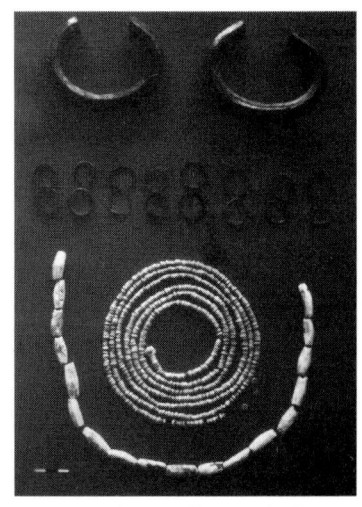

Figure 11.5b Jewellery made from heaps of empty shells, most of which heaps are used as quarries

Sites on the river Senegal

Abdoulaye Camara

Sites in the river valley have always been under threat from the Public Works Department. In 1958 gold bracelets and other items brought to light by workings at Podor led to the inhabitants digging in the surrounding area. IFAN could purchase only a few objects. Now, the sites are beginning to be destroyed with the creation of irrigated areas following the construction of the Diama dam and with the settlement of displaced people in the valley.

The simplest measures to adopt would be to give archaeologists money, whether from private or public sources, to enable them to carry out salvage excavations.[5]

Megalithic monuments

Megalithic monuments occupy the region between Kaolack and Tambacounda, an area stretching 250 km from east to west and 150 km from north to south. In Senegambia the current census lists 1,924 megalithic sites containing 16,320 monuments. These funerary monuments, dating from the second century BC to the sixteenth century AD, are of various types: megalithic circles, stone tumuli, stone circles and megalithic tumuli. These constructions, made of blocks of laterite stone, enclose skeletons (ranging from two to fifty-nine individuals) along with weapons and funerary furnishings. The laterite monuments are deteriorating as vegetation grows over them. The monoliths are also deteriorating from the effect of temperature changes. The most ornate monoliths, the famous 'stone lyres', are almost all broken and fallen down. Of forty-seven known stones, only three are still standing in the megalith area. International help would be required to put back up and stick together the fallen and broken blocks. One stone lyre was sent to the Musée national des arts africains et océaniens in Paris,[6] and another, from Soto (Kaffrine), was erected on private property in Dakar by the former director of the CGES in payment for services rendered. This latter monument could be returned at the request of the Senegalese authorities.

Certain provisions to ensure a degree of protection have been advocated:

1. The felling of trees within circles or growing into monoliths.

2. The planting of trees some way away from circles, so as to protect them from temperature variations.

3. Putting some monoliths back upright and sticking the broken ones together again.

Provisions have been adopted for some sites. Circles have been enclosed at Maka Gouye, Keur Ali Laobé, in 1968, at Delbi, Sorokone and Sine Ngayène. The system of enclosure used by the Directorate of the Historic and Ethnographic Heritage seems not to have yielded satisfactory results; enclosures are often too close to the monuments; fencing deteriorates rapidly; trellises, barbed wire and metal supports are taken by local people.

Tumuli

The tumuli area occupies the western half of Senegal and includes 1,444 sites containing 6,868 burial mounds or heaps of sand with base diameters ranging from a few metres to over 80 m. Two radiocarbon datings have given

783±116 AD for Ndalane (Kaolack region) and 1199±100 at Rao (near Saint-Louis). These funerary monuments, 1–4 m in height, also include furnishings comprising jewellery, weapons and terracotta objects.

Compared with other Iron Age sites, the threats hanging over these monuments are lesser but nevertheless real.

Provisions need to be taken:
1. To protect monuments that are situated in fields.
2. To see that roads follow a course away from major sites.

Figure 11.6a (*left*) Megalithic circle at Touba Loumpour. The village is built up against the monument which serves as a passageway for people and animals

Figure 11.6b (*right*) Lyre-stone taken from a megalithic site and now in a private garden in Dakar (*Photo: C. Descamps*)

The Senegalese heritage includes historic remains dating essentially from the nineteenth century, religious sites and natural sites.

Historic, natural and religious sites

Historic sites

Most of the sites preserved date from the period of colonial expansion. But very often the quality of materials used, combined with the rigours of the climate and lack of maintenance, has led to the disappearance of a number of old buildings.

Gorée. Many interests have pleaded for the preservation of this historic island. They were heard by the French colonial administrators very early on, leading to the promulgation of a number of regulations to conserve the site from demolition and disfiguration.[7] Gorée is one of the sites that UNESCO placed on the World Heritage List in September 1978.

Saint-Louis. The town of Saint-Louis, built in 1659, is one of the earliest European establishments in West Africa. Not having enjoyed the benefit of a good preservation policy like Gorée, many of its houses are in a bad way.

Figure 11.7a Megalithic circle at Koumpetoum, Tambacounda region. The monument is used as a rubbish dump. A baobab is now growing in the circle

Figure 11.7b Sine-Ngayène, Nioro region, is the largest megalithic grouping in Senegal with 523 circles and some 1,100 monoliths

Carabane. This town, the former capital of Casamance, includes early nineteenth-century buildings.

Apart from these historic islands, the Senegalese heritage includes:

Colonial military constructions, such as the forts at Bakel (1819), Dagana (1821), Mérinaghene on Lake Guiers (1822), Lampsar (1843), Sénoudébou

Towards a new policy to protect sites and monuments

Figure 11.8 Ruins of French fort at Sénoudébou, Tambacounda region

(1850), Podor (1854) and Sédhiou (1886) as well as others that have completely disappeared, like Matam (1857), Saldé (1859), etc.

Military constructions of a number of Senegalese freedom fighters: tatas (fortified enclosures) of Alpha Molo at Ndorma, Moussa Molo at Hamdallahi in Fuladu, Sada Bocar at Hamdallaye in Bundu, Alboury at Yang-Yang, etc.

Colonial residences such as the Palais de la République, the Ministry of Foreign Affairs, formerly the Palais de Justice (1905–59), the National Assembly, the Musée d'art africain, the town hall, the chamber of commerce, the Hôtel du gouvernement at Saint-Louis, Baron Roger's *château* at Richard Toll, the Ziguinchor Cultural Centre, etc.

Residences of Senegalese rulers or notables such as those of Bour Sine Coumba Ndoffène at Diakhao, Bouna Alboury at Yang-Yang, etc.

Battlefields such as Diallowali, Ngol Ngol, Dékhelé, etc.

Railway stations, as at Dakar, Rufisque, Thiès, Tivaouane, Saint-Louis, Tambacounda, etc.

Schools such as the Lycée Abdoulaye Sadji in Rufisque, the Ecole normale William Ponty at Sébikhotane, the Ecole normale William Ponty at Gorée.

Natural and religious sites

The Pointe des Almadies (17°32'30") is the westernmost point not only of Africa but of the entire Old World. Despite regulations dating from the colonial period classifying the Pointe des Almadies and the island of Ngor as natural sites[8] the area has been built on and developed.

Religious sites such as the mosques at Guédé, Pire, Touba, Tivaouane and Médina Wouro as well as mausoleums or cemeteries (e.g. of Maba Diakhou or the Almamys at Maboumba) and cathedrals (Dakar, Ziguinchor) are in a satisfactory state of conservation.

Figure 11.9 Ruins of villa of Bouna Alboury at Yang-Yang, Linguère department: the interior was used as a sheep pen

A new protection and conservation policy

It can be seen that the heritage is rich in archaeological remains of every period. It is important for us to protect them for the good of the whole community. *The listing of cultural treasures is only a first step and must lead to the protection, upkeep and hence the financing of protective measures.* Why, despite legislation, are the existing structures – the Directorate of the Cultural and Ethnographic Heritage, the Bureau of Architecture and Historic Monuments, the Institut Fondamental d'Afrique Noire – paralysed? Leaving aside the lack of co-ordination among these bodies, the causes are many: lack of logistics, absence of a fund to make emergency intervention possible on archaeological and historic sites, the permeability of our borders to the export of illicitly acquired cultural items.[9]

In the framework of the World Culture Decade, IFAN and the Directorate of the Historic and Ethnographic Heritage put to the Ministry of Culture a document listing the factors threatening the heritage and suggesting measures to be taken to protect and conserve it.

Measures of co-operation to promote dialogue among historians, archaeologists and the public services about archaeological inventories. Such measures should include:

1. Involving IFAN–Ch. A. Diop in the protection activities of the Directorate of the Historic and Ethnographic Heritage of the Ministry of Culture.

2. Reviving the Commission supérieure des monuments historiques.

3. Adopting another list of sites and monuments with a view to their listing.

4. Setting aside a budget managed by IFAN–Ch. A. Diop for emergency intervention on threatened archaeological sites (salvage excavations, for example).

Figure 11.10 William Ponty School at Sébikotane where many African leaders were trained

Working methods must be improved by:
1. Equipping archaeologists and historians, as well as others with expertise relevant to the physical heritage, with the means to obtain new equipment and take advantage of new methods of conserving and protecting cultural property.
2. Developing the restoration and preservation facilities of IFAN–Ch. A. Diop, which has significant collections in its stores that are archives of the past.
3. Promoting the opening of workshop schools for the training of technicians working in existing research institutions and students.
4. Giving co-ordinators, museum curators, research technicians and students scholarships to enable them to specialize in conserving and restoring the heritage.

A variety of activities to raise awareness and educate the public (through broadcasts in national languages, documentary films, handbooks, pamphlets) must be aimed at public opinion to encourage the protection of the heritage and the enhancement of cultures and cultural property. In this framework, the Commission supérieure des monuments historiques, the Directorate of Tourism Promotion, the Post Office, museums and research institutions, etc., might:
1. Publish pamphlets, stamps, posters and calendars showing sites and objects of cultural interest.
2. Publish articles on topics touching on the physical heritage in the national and international press, in magazines aimed at tourists and in those of airlines.
3. Mount light exhibitions of tourism and cultural information, encourage the public to discover the richness of its heritage and show it the conservation measures adopted at the national level.

4. Organize meetings on topics related to the conservation of the cultural heritage.

A document under the auspices of the Commission supérieure des monuments historiques and IFAN–Ch. A. Diop might set out each year:

1. The state of the classification of sites, conservation measures adopted and solutions expected.
2. Tour routes of sites of cultural interest, museums and 'small site museums' associated with cultural remains *in situ*.
3. The conservation actions taken by big companies, notably development and construction services whose activities may harm sites.
4. The sources of funding and the intervention funds for salvage archaeology.

Notes

1. Ministerial order No. 3943 PM/MC of 18 May 1979.
2. Ministerial orders No. 6876 of 19 August 1991, containing publication of the list of historic monuments and sites, and No. 1146 of 30 January 1992, containing proposals for listing.
3. Some 1,924 sites containing 16,320 monuments.
4. This is true also of the shell middens at Saloum and the *mbanars* in the Diourbel region. The measures in force to protect some sites are paid scant regard. (The Khang marigot neolithic industry in the Saint-Louis region has disappeared completely.)
5. It is in this context that a major exhibition programme is being conducted by the IFAN–Ch. A. Diop prehistory and protohistory laboratory.
6. Franco-Senegalese protocol of 31 May 1967. In accordance with article 4 of the protocol 'These deposits are loans for a period of three years, which may be tacitly renewed in accordance with the standards adopted by the International Commission on Museums (ICOM–UNESCO, note 3)'.
7. Decree of 25 August 1937 (*Journal officiel,* p. 1063), promulgated by order No. 2805/AP of 16 October 1937, on the protection of national monuments and sites of a historical character under a mandate from the Colonial Ministry; order of 15 November 1944 (*Journal officiel,* p. 403) setting up a Commission des monuments historiques et des arts indigènes which in turn was the origin of the subsequent order; order of 15 February 1951 (*Journal officiel,* p. 234) in its articles 36.1–3 declaring Gorée a 'historic site' and envisaging the establishment of a special commission to examine requests for permission to do work there.
8. Order No. 2223 of 10 August 1942 (*Journal officiel,* p. 717).
9. Departure controls at airports are ineffective and lack of training means that customs officers are unable to differentiate between an antiquity and a modern copy.

References

Archives du Laboratoire de préhistoire–protohistoire de l'IFAN.
Becker, C. and Martin, V. 1973. *Historique des recherches sur la protohistoire sénégambienne.* Kaolack, roneo.
Bessac, H. 1953. 'Découverte de Paléolithique évolué à Richard-Toll (Bas Sénégal)', *Notes africaines* 59, 65–67.

Camara, A. 1984. *Le Paléolithique au Sénégal: carte d'identité des monuments du Sénégal.* Direction du Patrimoine National, No. 1, June, pp. 37–44.

Chavane, B. 1985. *Village de l'ancien Tekrour: recherches archéologiques dans la moyenne vallée du fleuve Sénégal.* Paris: Karthala-CRA.

Descamps, C. 1969. 'Note sur le néolithique du Sénégal', *Bulletin du ASEQUA* 22, 35–37.

—— 1971. *Rapport préliminaire sur la fouille de Dioron-Boumak (Sine-Saloum), 9 mars au 15 avril 1971.* Dakar.

—— 1972. 'Contribution à la préhistoire de l'Ouest Sénégalais'. Thesis, Université de Paris I. Travaux et documents, Département d'histoire, Faculté des lettres et sciences humaines, Université de Dakar, II, 1979.

—— 1982. *La Préhistoire au Sénégal.* Dakar: Association sénégalaise des professeurs d'histoire et géographie.

Gosnave, D., Fall, B. and Gaye, D. 1988. *Sites et monuments en Sénégambie: images et esquisses historiques.* Dakar: Association des professeurs d'histoire et géographie.

Joie, J. 1955. 'Découvertes archéologiques dans la région de Rao (bas-Sénégal)', *Bulletin de l'IFAN* B, XVII (3–4), 249–333.

Mauny, R. 1961. *Tableau géographique de l'Ouest africain au Moyen-age.* Dakar: IFAN.

Thilmans, G. 1977. 'Sur les objets de parure trouvés à Podor (Sénégal)', *Bull. IFAN* B, 39, (4), 669–94.

Thilmans, G., Descamps, C. and Khayat, B. 1980. *Protohistoire du Sénégal* I, *Les sites mégalithiques.* Dakar: IFAN.

Thilmans, G. and Ravise, A. 1983. *Protohistoire du Sénégal* II, *Recherches archéologiques II, Sintiou-Bara et les sites du fleuve.* Dakar: IFAN.

12 Niger
The Case of the Musée National

MARIAMA HIMA
Musée National du Niger, Niamey

Overview of the Musée national

The Musée National du Niger, covering an area of 24.3 ha, came into being on 18 December 1959, with the break-up of the IFAN centre attached to the Institut Fondamental d'Afrique Noire into the Centre national de recherches en sciences humaines and the museum. It comes under the Ministry of Communication, Culture, Youth and Sport. From its foundation the institution operated without any formal legal instrument until the adoption of presidential decree No. 90256/PRN/MJC/C of 28 December 1990 making the Musée national an 'administrative public institution' enjoying financial semi-autonomy. It is administered by a curator and employs a total of seventy-four staff of all categories.

The Musée national du Niger is a multidisciplinary type of museum devoted to every aspect of the cultural and natural life of Niger. It includes a number of exhibition spaces and technical units:

1. The Classical Hall, or Pavillon Boubou Hama, built in 1959 for an exhibition of ethnographic and archaeological objects.
2. The Musical Instrument Hall.
3. The Traditional Costume Hall.
4. The Open Air Museum, where features of traditional architecture are recreated.
5. The Palaeontology and Prehistory Hall.
6. The Archaeology Hall.
7. The Mausoleum of the Tree of Ténéré.
8. The Uranium Hall.
9. The Zoological Park.
10. The Garden of Nations.
11. The Rock Carving Exhibition Hall, containing the museum's store.
12. The Audio-visual Hall, altered into a temporary exhibition hall.
13. The photographic laboratory.

In addition to its tasks of conservation and restoration the museum has become involved in educational and social activities, which have led to the development of the following services:

The educational centre, set up in 1970 to teach children expelled from primary school manual activities in specialized workshops: batik, welding, carpentry, plumbing, building, electricity, needlework.

The craft centre, set up in 1959–60: craftsmen from all over the country carry on smithing, jewellery-making, weaving, pottery-making, leather-working, carving, etc.

The workshop for the disabled, set up in 1972 to train disabled children in shoemaking so that they might live without begging.

Archaeological research

Although Niger's archaeological importance was highlighted as long ago as 1909, research in this area only really got under way around 1930, with the collections gathered during military patrols in the Azawak, Aïr and Ténéré areas. The collections were sent for study either to the Musée de l'homme in Paris or to the Institut français de l'Afrique noire in Dakar.

It was not until 1959, with the creation of the Musée national, that Niger had an institution in which archaeological material could be housed. Archaeological research itself began to come under national control only in 1966, with the creation of the archaeological section of what was to become the Centre Nigérien de Recherches en Sciences Humaines (CNRSH) which in 1974 became the Institut de Recherches en Sciences Humaines of the Université de Niamey (IRSH). The sums allocated to archaeological research are so small that the buildings have never been adapted to the requirements of a proper archaeological laboratory and repository.

However, the installation of the ORSTOM laboratory in 1976 partly freed some of the space at the IRSH by housing the collections built up by researchers while they were being studied. Another storage centre was formed with the creation of a repository for finds at Agadez during an archaeological salvage programme in the Igall–Teggiden'Tessum region, a Franco-Nigérien project (CNRS–IRSH–ORSTOM).

The existence of the three institutions (IRSH, ORSTOM, Musée national) makes it possible to manage archaeological objects in such a way that the public can see them. The complementary roles of the institutions should make it possible to carry out almost all aspects of the processing of archaeological material.

Archaeological research is very much alive in Niger. Unfortunately, a lack of on-going co-ordination militates against a national policy to conserve and enhance collections.

The museum's archaeological collections

When the Musée national was established in Niamey in 1959 it was situated in the former premises of the IFAN centre with a few existing archaeological and ethnographic collections. The archaeological collections consisted mainly of pottery, millstones and stone arrowheads. Starting from his own experience of archaeological excavations in Tunisia on the site of Carthage, the founder of the museum, Pablo Toucet, had, from the beginning, combined archaeological research on the ground and the development of the Musée national.

In 1959 and 1960 he undertook archaeological excavations on the site of Tondikoiré, near Tamalé and near Torodi. The pottery he collected was put on display and on deposit in the Classical Hall. Palaeontological research carried out at the Musée d'histoire naturelle in Paris under the aegis of Philippe

Tacquet led to the exhibition of the cranium of the crocodilian *Sarcosuchus imperator* in the Classical Hall, and later the creation of the Palaeontology Hall and the exhibition of a fossil tree trunk in the late 1960s and early 1970s.

This was followed by building the hall for the deposit of ethnographic collections in which reproductions and photographs of rock carvings and paintings were exhibited side by side, mostly the work of Jean-Pierre Roset of ORSTOM.

The Nigérien Prehistory and Archaeology Hall came into being in 1980, offering the public a glimpse of the results of research carried out by teams from the Université de Niamey and ORSTOM, especially the work done in Djado and Kawar by Thierry Tillet on the Old Stone Age, in the Aïr and the Ténéré by Jean-Pierre Roset and François Paris on the Late Stone Age rock art and burial places and in the Niger valley by Boube Gado on the proto-historical and historical period.

Yet, for lack of logistical and financial means, the Musée national has not fully benefited from the results of the major excavations and discoveries that have been made in Niger. In 1993 the 'Vallées du Niger' international exhibition benefited fully from them, presenting terracotta figurines from the river valley and pottery and textiles from the Aïr.

The lay public and the scientific public

The various halls of the museum have always been much loved by the public. Among the Nigérien public the archaeological collections evoke more curiosity and astonishment than understanding of the message of the exhibitions themselves, when they are not linked up to the universe of story and myth, as was the case with a piece of fossil rock displayed near the 100 million-year-old silicified tree trunk, the same age as the cranium of the *Sarcosuchus imperator* displayed in the Boubou Hama Hall.

In addition to the scholarly public passing through to visit the collections on display, the latter were used by students at the Niamey Institut régional de muséologie for their practical work, their exhibitions and their guided tours. Guided tours are also organized for schools, from primary level upwards. But the most important exhibition is the one devoted to Niger's past. It stretches over a vast period from the Old Stone Age to the sixteenth century.

Legal and institutional problems

The management of the archaeological heritage, a vulnerable part of the cultural heritage, generally poses legal and institutional problems in Africa. The Republic of Niger does not escape the gaps, shortcomings and contradictions of laws and regulations or the difficulties of applying or interpreting them. The consequences are important and create risks for archaeological collections. For the management of the archaeological heritage requires as its starting point that objects should be well conserved. The law must come to the help of culture by creating a suitable regulatory framework to protect and exploit archaeological material. A quick analysis of the situation in Niger highlights the following gaps:

1. The absence of satisfactory legal provisions governing research in general and archaeological excavations in particular.

2. The absence of adequate legal provision for the protection of the cultural heritage, in particular the classification of historic monuments and buildings (except for the Aïr Ténéré and the Parc du W, which are on the World Heritage List as natural sites).

3. The lack of co-ordination between national institutions responsible for protecting the cultural heritage.

In reality the status of collections is dealt with and settled amicably by the Ministry responsible for higher education and research and the Ministry of Culture, often with the involvement of the Ministry of the Interior. The basic principle is that every archaeological object discovered within the country belongs absolutely to the Nigérien state. More appropriate legal provision is expected to be promulgated soon.

However, over and beyond problems of administrative co-ordination, the museologist's prime concern is to know what the archaeologist wants when he entrusts his object to the curator.

13 Cape Verde
Site & Archaeological Heritage Conservation at Cidade Velha

NELIDA MARIA LIMA RODRIGUES
National Institute of Culture, Praia

Although Cape Verde as yet lacks any concrete museum infrastructure, a number of projects are currently being carried out. At independence the country inherited no museum or suchlike institution, nor any provision for conservation. Nor could it envisage them as a priority during the first years of national reconstruction, given the urgency of immediate social action in such areas as food, health and basic education in a low-income country. Today, however, we can say that action is being taken to conserve our cultural assets.

Proposals for museums and the archaeological heritage have been initiated in various parts of the country, although they have not yet really taken off because of the shortage of human and financial resources. They have helped to develop a policy for training personnel, both at the national level and abroad.

Some of them are developing under the aegis of the National Cultural Institute (INAC). Such is the case with proposals for a National Museum of Cultural History at Praia and a site museum at 'Cidade Velha'. Both are of great importance to the conservation of our cultural heritage. At present, however, priority is given to conservation of the site of Cidade Velha, where study of the archaeological heritage should enable us to deepen our knowledge of our roots and our evolution as a people and to become more firmly aware of our cultural heritage.

Adoption of cultural legislation

The most important action undertaken by the state has been, on the one hand, to create infrastructures and, on the other, to take measures to promote conservation and organization in this area.

The adoption of basic cultural legislation is one of the first steps in that direction. More particularly, the law adopted in 1990, with its object as 'the conservation, defence and enhancement of the Cape Verdean cultural heritage', defines this latter as 'consisting of all the material and immaterial items which, by virtue of their intrinsic value, must be considered of major interest for conserving identity and enhancing Cape Verdean culture over time'. The law protects 'material property', 'movable property', 'historic monuments', 'historic sites' and 'architectural groupings'. That is essential to conserve Cidade Velha in all its aspects, the most important of which, however, is the local population.

Figure 13.1 View of part of Cidade Velha

The law also requires the state 'to preserve, defend and enhance the cultural heritage of the Cape Verdean people, by inducing them to create and promote the conditions necessary to do so'. It is also interesting that the law places upon local authorities identical obligations regarding the heritage situated within the bounds of their jurisdiction.

Listing of cultural property is planned, which makes for a higher degree of protection, given the obligation to carry out works on listed property.

While the law is well drawn up in terms of its conception and the duties assigned to institutions and the public in the interests of conserving and enhancing the cultural and historical heritage, it has to be pointed out that it has not yet been implemented for want of machinery to enforce it. The reason is largely lack of resources, especially trained manpower. In practice, efforts are being made, using existing resources with the backing of the law, to secure the means of attaining the objectives sought. Thus it has been possible to advance the Cidade Velha project thanks above all to the personal commitment of a number of individuals (members of the government, heads of public cultural institutions) who have helped to draw upon the site the attention it deserves.

Cidade Velha and its history

Cape Verde is an archipelago some 900 km off the north-west coast of the African continent, and it owes its foundation to the Cidade Velha (old city), initially called Ribeira Grande, on the island of Santiago. The islands were discovered in 1460 by the Portuguese, who began populating them in 1462 with slaves brought from the African continent and with Europeans, the archipelago being then uninhabited, according to the official version of events.

Figure 13.2 The remains of the walls of Cidade Velha

Ribeira Grande was the first centre of population in Cape Verde, and the first city built by the Portuguese in Africa. Its elevation to the status of city dates from 1533. It was then that the first diocese was set up in Cape Verde.

The historical and cultural value of the city cannot be denied, testimony as it is of a whole dynamic that developed at a specific moment in world history when Europe expanded into new lands. The Cape Verde archipelago, particularly the city of Ribeira Grande, played an important role as a principal focus of activity in the Atlantic, on the route between Europe, Africa and America, first in the adventure of the discoveries and then in the slave trade and trade generally. During the sixteenth century almost all the Atlantic trade routes passed through Ribeira Grande, which led the Portuguese Crown to equip the city with a minimum of infrastructure to enable it to oversee that traffic.

From the very beginning this prosperity attracted pirates and a few navigators made famous by history, as well as adventurers and corsairs who passed through the island's port. But, perhaps more important, not only African slaves of various ethnic backgrounds but cultivated plants, technologies and animals also passed through Ribeira Grande, for acclimatization before being taken on to such countries as Brazil or the West Indies. Various races and languages met and mixed there, leading some writers to describe the site as a 'cultural laboratory'.

If the rise of the city was rapid, its fall was no less so. Several factors explain the decline, such as the unhealthiness of the area, the loss of the monopoly of trade and the tax on slaves, the weakness of its defence capacity and the frequent attacks by pirates and corsairs, such as the one in 1585 by English privateers commanded by Francis Drake in the service of the English Crown, and in 1712 by French pirates commanded by Jacques Cassard,

Site & Archaeological Heritage Conservation at Cidade Velha

Figure 13.3 Ruins of the Cathedral

during which the city was ransacked and completely destroyed. In 1769 the seat of government was transferred to the city of Praia.

The site museum project

This whole past is given explicit material form by the archaeological and architectural remains that survive despite the neglect from which they have long suffered. For lack of means, or from ignorance of the cultural value of the site, the population that grew up there contributed largely to the ruin of a great number of buildings, using the stones to build their own houses.

The site received little attention from the Portuguese colonial authorities. It was only during the 1960s, on the occasion of the commemoration of the Portuguese maritime discoveries, that work was carried out on conserving some moments. Today there are grounds for asking how wisely the work was carried out. In some cases the original features of monuments have completely disappeared, and the materials used, such as concrete, are not the most suitable ones. Caritas, a religious institution, carried out some restoration work but with no real direction. All these moves aimed at reconstructing buildings with modern materials, eliminating much of the architectural evidence beforehand. Fortunately the archaeological remains in the ground suffered no great damage, which is why they can be studied now.

The first archaeological work carried out in Cape Verde was on Cidade Velha cathedral, a building today in ruins. The work was carried out in two stages. First the interior was cleared and superficially excavated (with digging where necessary), then architectural features that were part of the structure of the building were recovered, and some graves found during the work were excavated. What the excavations produced was fragments of African pottery (although it has not yet been possible to identify their cultural provenance),

Figure 13.4 (*left*) Ruins of the tower of the Church of Mercy

Figure 13.5 (*right*) The Church of Our Lady of Rosario

Portuguese china and Chinese earthenware, as well as human bones, often buried in groups of more than two. The material has yet to be adequately processed, apart from being cleaned, sorted and given a preliminary classification. We are hoping to create the conditions for the material to be studied so that it can be shown to the public. The first stage was accompanied by partial consolidation of some of the walls with a view to further rehabilitation later. Before the monument is restored a third and last stage, excavating the remaining graves, is planned, preceding the placing of plates and other structural features.

Other archaeological work is planned in various places and buildings in Cidade Velha such as the Fort of S. Verissimo, the Tower of the Church of Mercy and the City Gate, as soon as it can all be arranged. In addition, one-off archaeological surveys are carried out in places regarded as being in danger, as when building sites are started. All this work has been documented archaeologically and museographically, using audio-visual equipment, so as to provide a basis for study and, above all, background information for the public.

All this had led to the constitution of a significant archaeological collection – the first in Cape Verde – which is kept in the technical department of the INAC at Cidade Velha, until such time as conditions are right for it to be studied, conserved and restored, allowing it then to be displayed. On the basis of this holding it is planned to set up a Museum of History, probably in one of the restored parts of the cathedral.

Among the activities to promote museum structures supporting archaeological conservation, work has begun on restoring a ruined house to accommodate a small local museum. It is intended that it will reproduce the environment of a traditional dwelling, as an example of how the ruins of small people's houses can be converted, retaining the architectural appearance

Site & Archaeological Heritage Conservation at Cidade Velha

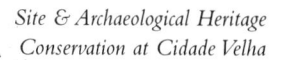

Figure 13.6 The Royal Fort of St. Philip

and historical context. An archaeological survey is under way as a prelude to restoration. The museographical collection will be assembled at the end of this stage.

Thus the approach adopted consists of making archaeological investigation the basis of all restoration and rehabilitation work, with a view to acquiring better knowledge of the site so that conservation is always conceived in a global framework.

As part and parcel of the same approach, other steps are being taken, put together by experts in various disciplines. A bureau has been set up, drawing in all the experts of the National Cultural Institute (archaeologists, a museum expert, an anthropologist and a sociologist) and of the municipality of Praia (an architect, designers and a social worker). The bureau is working on a larger-scale proposal, based on the conception of a site museum, designed to conserve the site as a whole. The conservation of monuments and archaeological research is conceived in tandem with other large-scale measures, such as controls upon building in the historical area and the adjoining area, improving the local population's living conditions and creating tourist facilities.

This approach has been reasserted by the town planning architect assigned by UNESCO, who came to Cape Verde on a consultation exercise to draw up a master plan for the archaeological heritage. Since 1980 several missions of this nature have come and gone. Unfortunately they have produced only written reports, with no practical consequences, which is chiefly due to lack of resources.

Following these missions, application was made in 1990 for Cidade Velha to be added to the World Heritage List, but without success; the minimum working conditions required for the conservation of the site could not be met. The attitude at the time was in fact to seek rather to focus attention on the monuments.

UNESCO's recommendations were followed in order to compile as full a dossier as possible: Cidade Velha was declared a national heritage site; an inventory of existing monuments was carried out; the law on the conservation, defence and enhancement of the Cape Verdean heritage was published. Despite these efforts, in 1992 UNESCO again rejected the application on the grounds that the conditions had not been met. The National Cultural Institute is therefore continuing its efforts to promote the candidacy of Cidade Velha, laying greater stress on the monument/environment/population nexus.

A draft proposal is being considered regarding the 'integral rehabilitation' of Cidade Velha. This study was carried out by a Spanish firm, Arcotech, at the request of the National Cultural Institute on the basis of ideas put forward by national experts.

The INAC and the municipality of Praia Bureau are jointly endeavouring to be more efficient. The fact that the staff assigned to the bureau are involved in various other national projects in other parts of the country does not make the task any easier.

Archaeological programmes need to be developed both for site excavations and for submarine and industrial archaeology. The submarine archaeology of the bay that surrounds Cidade Velha, for example, would considerably enhance research into the city. However, it would require a level of investment and specialist personnel that is beyond our means. As for industrial archaeology, there are significant remains that ought to be conserved, but the human resources are insufficient – museum experts, researchers.

The difficulty of training specialists is one handicap: Cape Verde has no university and lacks suitably equipped research centres. The fact that the country is an archipelago creates many other problems, including isolation and the need to distribute resources (human resources in particular) among the islands, so as to meet needs and requests of different parts of the country.

To conclude, it emerges from all that has been set out that we are still only just beginning, that the difficulties are many and the resources scarce. But we are trying to make the most of what we have and even to turn our weaknesses into strengths. If we can start from this principle to plan our actions well and benefit from the experience of those who began long before us and if we can unite our efforts on an interdisciplinary basis to improve our programmes, our path will surely be easier.

PART III

Communication & Education

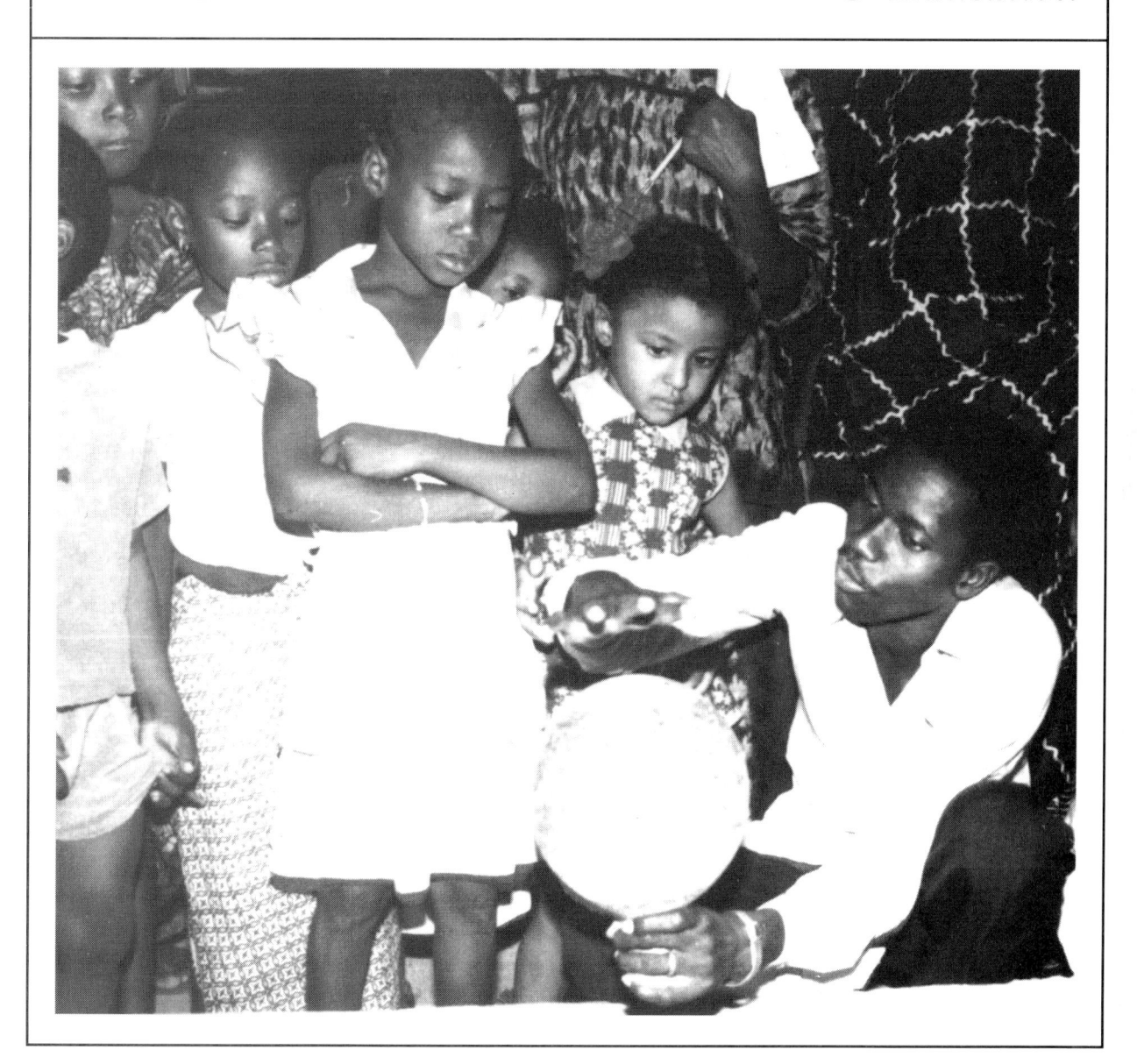

14 Burkina Faso
Archaeological Information, Education & Museums

ALMISSI PORGO
Direction du patrimoine culturel, Ouagadougou

The upheavals that have occurred in Africa have sorely tested traditions and contributed to the uprootedness of many Africans. The latter are in quest of their identity. The results of archaeological research can partly help to resolve the problem, provided that this precious and important information is made available to the public. The museum, as an instrument of education and dissemination, must play its role by returning archaeological objects and information to the public whose inheritance they are.

Unfortunately, attempts to do so are for the time being timid. This chapter examines the case of Burkina Faso. After a general survey it looks at the prospects offered in the framework of the new national museum.

The current situation

Archaeological research in Burkina Faso is the responsibility of the Université de Ouagadougou, mainly the Department of History and Archaeology of the Faculty of Letters and Human Sciences. Work undertaken in recent years has led to the collection of a rich archaeological heritage which is managed by the archaeology laboratory of the university.

The Musée national for its part has a small archaeological collection, put together by researchers who have worked with the museum. Action has been undertaken by museologists and archaeologists to make this heritage available to the public:

1. *Study visits to the field*. Teachers of archaeology at the university endeavour on every occasion to associate the Department of Cultural Heritage with study visits to the field.

2. *Research*. Several categories of objects from the collections of the national museum have been analysed in theses by archaeology students.

3. *Organization of exhibitions*. The national museum has accommodated exhibitions organized by archaeologists or historians. An example was the 'Archéologie au Burkina Faso' exhibition organized by the History and Archaeology Club.

The museum's exhibitions have been enriched by the contribution of works from the archaeological research of the archaeology laboratory. The funerary vases used in the exhibition 'La porterie dans la société traditionelle burkinabé' (1990) were made available to the museum by the laboratory. But such instances are few and far between. The many possibilities are underexploited.

Yet the case of the village museum at Pobé Mengao can serve as an example of how the museum can return objects to the community and provide the public with archaeological information.

The village museum of Pobé Mengao

The village of Pobé Mengao lies in northern Burkina Faso 30 km southwest of Djibo on the Djibo–Ouahigouya road in the province of Soum (Gérard, 1990). Pobé Mengao is the capital of Lorum, a Kurumfe state. Lurum was a place where nomadic and sedentary populations met: Kurumba, Dogon, Nyoryosa, Moose, Songhaï and Fulbe. The Kurumba were the founders of the state of Lurum. When they arrived in Lurum they found the remains of earlier occupation. Today the archaeological remains of Lurum are:

1. Granite rock carvings;
2. Small man-made mounds, their surfaces covered with pottery fragments and lithic materials;
3. Small man-made mounds with vases in a horizontal position;
4. Iron production sites.

Pobé Mengao is an important archaeological site which has attracted both national and foreign researchers. Among them a French archaeologist, Bertrand Gérard, was the initiator of the construction of the village museum at Pobé Mengao, which he planned. Uniquely in Burkina Faso the Pobé Mengao museum was built and run by local people, with the help of Bertrand Gérard, without the intervention of the Musée national or the administrative authorities. The building was completed in 1979 and has mud walls and floors. It is supervised by the archaeology laboratory of the Department of History and Archaeology of the Université de Ouagadougou.

The museum's collections deal with the 'prehistory and history' of Lurum. Bertrand Gérard deposited in it all the objects collected by him and his team. The bulk of the collection consists of pottery. There are also ploughing implements, headdresses, staffs, statuettes, masks and leatherwork. All the objects come either from the immediate neighbourhood of the village or from places that tradition attributes to the old state. For Bertrand Gérard, 'by the forms, characteristics and decorative motifs associated with them, their provenance and their being assembled in one place they constitute a system of signs that lends support to and underlines the story told by a tradition of which the elders are the keepers'.

The Pobé Mengao museum is an example of returning archaeological objects and information to their place of origin. But it may be wondered whether a museum has any place in village society. The answer is yes. Bertrand Gérard sees in his achievement a necessity. The museum meets the major concerns of the inhabitants of the village. 'If the chief and I decided to set up in this place, it was indeed because the voice of Lorum had fallen silent. This museum would in future be a place where the elders could speak of the old Lorum and pass the signs of it on to the children from the state school and the Koranic school in the village' (Gérard, 1990). The museum thus becomes a school where education is an important extra feature.

The museum seeks to be an integral part of the village: 'It is not in the name of some need to preserve the "material evidence" of the past history of Lorum that we took the decision to build this "house". Bringing these objects together became possible and desired only when the gradual loss of language and tradition was regarded as irreversible. The bringing together of characteristic objects of Kurumba culture was seen as giving young people access to a place where the elders, referring to the sequence of objects, how they are aligned and arranged, could pass on their knowledge. This museum is neither a mosque nor an ancestral hut but a public place where Muslims and traditionalists, old and young, can meet without compromising the principles that elsewhere keep them apart.'

The village museum of Pobé Mengao ought thus to meet the needs of the people. It is the fruit of archaeological research. It is desirable that the example should be followed in order to save what can be saved of our cultural heritage at a time when we are witnessing systematic pillage of archaeological sites and a haemorrhaging of the cultural heritage.

In Burkina Faso the results of research in general and of archaeology in particular will be the foundations on which the new national museum will be constructed.

Prospects

The Musée national has existed in Burkina Faso since 1962. But it has never been able to play its full role as a cultural focus. Now it is planned to build a new museum. Optimal use of this cultural resource requires an appropriate communication strategy, which implies having a global vision of the questions of communication and education.

What type of communication?

Unlike information, which is data conveyed to a person or a group irrespective of his or its reaction, communication is a relationship between two persons or two groups (here the museum and its public). To communicate is thus to enter into relations 'with . . .'. The message which connects them must therefore be of interest to both parties. The factors that determine the nature of the message are: the target public, the aims of the message; its content, its functions and its form.

Museums must try to present messages that are direct, simple and capable of simultaneously informing, educating and motivating. That means messages that are well structured, well put together and which take account of the psychological, cultural and social factors inherent in their content.

Like every African country, Burkina Faso is replete with opportunities of communication. Musical instruments and the human voice are the most traditional. Africa is above all a continent in which orality is highly developed. Hence the need for museums to use national languages. National languages are one of the most effective means of asserting cultural identity. They facilitate access to knowledge and give the individual the feeling of belonging to a group. It is all the more important for our museums to take orality into account because captions, labels and other forms of written information are incomprehensible to the vast majority (nearly 90 per cent) of national publics. The public finds itself excluded from the museum, which it regards, rightly, as an area reserved for a socio-cultural elite. The museum must be able to make the transmission of knowledge an affective experience.

Education

Museum education is a process intended above all to stimulate the interest of the public (whether an individual or a group) and induce it to seek information and reflect on the solution to its problems. It is thus not a matter of overwhelming the public with information that appears useful. The museum is not solely a means of extending and complementing formal education. It must also be capable of attracting the attention of the average person, educated or not. Museums must endeavour to educate by entertaining.

The new Musée national in Burkina Faso

Shaping an image of the museum among Burkinabe is a great challenge in a country which lacks a museum culture. Modern and traditional means of communication must be resorted to and the whole population involved.

Exhibiting remains the optimal way for the museum to communicate with its public. It is planned to organize temporary, permanent and travelling exhibitions in which an attempt will be made to avoid this physical compartmentalization of related disciplines. This approach is dictated by the need to transmit a clear and structured educational and cultural message, accessible to a diverse public. The main topics focused on are:

1. Knowledge of the physical environment;
2. Archaeology and history;
3. Ethnography;
4. Rural activities and the habitat.

These exhibitions will be mounted in collaboration with all the archaeologists and other scholars whose work can help the museum play its role better.

The museum will organize workshops which will be essentially addressed to schools, while not excluding the possibility of carrying on educational activities directed at adults and young people who have received no education. The workshop programme will be arranged on a rotating basis which will alter in the light of the reactions and responses of participants.

Conclusion

Today, in an ever-changing world, it is more than ever necessary for archaeologists, museologists, historians, geographers, linguists and other resource persons to combine their energies and promote knowledge of our cultural identity.

This discussion has not touched on all the questions raised by communication and education in museums in relation to archaeology. But it is one contribution to a debate which, it is to be hoped, will be fruitful and beneficial for all concerned.

Reference

Gérard, Bertrand. 1990. 'Le Musée de Pobé Mengao, Burkina Faso', *Bulletin de l'Association française des anthropologues* 39, 77–81.

15 Mali
Opening the Musée National to Schools

SEYDOU OUATTARA

Musée national du Mali, Bamako

The Musée national du Mali is a public institution entrusted with the task of collecting, protecting, conserving and disseminating the national cultural heritage.

The idea of creating an ethnographic museum in the Sudan goes back to 1917. But it took concrete shape only in 1950 with the establishment of an embryonic museum in the Maison des artisans soudanais. The Musée soudanais was inaugurated on 14 February 1953 in provisional buildings at the Ecole des travaux publics (now the Ecole nationale d'ingénieurs) and in 1957 moved into its own premises. It was then part of the Institut Français d'Afrique Noire (IFAN). It became the Musée national du Mali at independence and in 1962 was placed under the Institut des sciences humaines, under the Ministry of National Education.

In 1975 its premises were taken away for use as a management training institute, and in 1976 the museum was attached to the Ministry of Youth, Sport, Arts and Culture. In 1980 two things happened that were important for the Musée national du Mali: its premises were restored to it and the first stone was laid of a new museum complex on the same site. The new museum, a fruit of Franco-Malian co-operation, was inaugurated on 8 March 1982.

It is currently responsible to the Ministry of Culture and Communication and includes, in addition to the administration, four technical sections: documentation and research, conservation and restoration, audio-visual and exhibition–outreach.

The Musée national du Mali: a brief introduction

The responsibilities assigned to the Musée national du Mali include support for public education through illustrating school syllabuses, co-operation with teachers, lending objects, preparing documents and organizing visits, among other things. To that end, in 1983, the museum addressed a letter of information to education inspectors and heads of educational establishments in the cities of Bamako and Kati. Following this first approach visits were made to a number of basic and higher education establishments in Bamako and in Fana, 110 km from Bamako.

In 1984 a start was made to putting our relations with educational establishments in Bamako and the surrounding area on a proper footing. The

The introduction of archaeology into the museum's educational programmes

Figure 15.1 Terracotta vessels from Timbuktu region, *ca.* 10th century (*Photo: Musée National du Mali*)

exhibition–outreach section was restructured. In the same year, at the request of the management of the Musée national, Miss Wassila Soussi, outreach worker at the Musée du Bardo in Tunis, paid a technical support visit to Bamako, financed by the Cultural and Technical Co-operation Agency (ACCT). The purpose of the mission was to ensure basic training for the staff of the section and to help draw up a programme for opening up the museum to schools.

A working party consisting of five artists (visual arts, music, dramatic arts) and two socio-cultural outreach workers was formed around the Tunisian co-ordinator. After drawing up a work schedule, contacts were made with the management of basic and vocational schools in Bamako as well with the Centre de rééducation pour les handicapés physiques (Centre for the Re-education of the Physically Handicapped), the Association malienne pour la promotion sociale des aveugles (Malian Association for the Social Advancement of the Blind) and a children's nursery in the city.

Following these meetings, the team detected major educational gaps in the syllabuses of these establishments as regards the content of the information, the language in which it was couched and above all the educational illustration of some of the lessons taught in class. In particular, those dealing with archaeology were the most inadequate and the most unacceptable.

The gaps were glaring because archaeology is included in the official history syllabuses of the fifth and sixth years of the first cycle of basic education, the seventh year of the second cycle of basic education, the tenth year of technical and vocational general secondary education and the first year of history and geography in the Ecole normale supérieure (teacher training college).

They were unacceptable because Mali is an ancient land which, from the most remote past, has seen several great civilizations rise and fall. Moreover there are in Mali itself research and information institutions such as the Institut des Sciences Humaines and the Musée national. It should also be stressed that the Musée national places great emphasis on archaeological exhibitions. Since its inauguration in 1982 it has organized four such exhibitions:

1982. 'Survol de l'archéologie malienne', with the help of the Institut des sciences humaines.

1985. 'Du Sahel au Sahara: le nord du Mali depuis 10.000 ans', with the assistance of the French Ministry of Co-operation.

1987. 'Archéologie du Mali' (continuing), with the assistance of the Institut des Sciences Humaines.

1991. 'Fanfannyègèné: un abri sous rocher dans le Baoulé il y a 3.000 ans', with the assistance of the embassy of the Federal Republic of Germany in Mali.

Given the importance and place of archaeology in school syllabuses, its treatment became the prime concern of the team headed by Miss Wassila Soussi. Our aim was not to take the place of teachers, but to make the teaching aid of the Musée national available to pupils and students by complementing the school syllabus on archaeology through illustrations.

Approach and working methods

In the concern to help pupils and students to understand their courses better, the Musée national offers teachers a series of in-house activities that are sometimes continued in educational institutions. The activities also enable those involved to get to know the wealth of the national cultural heritage. They are offered in the course of contact between outreach workers and educationalists from the museum and school managers in their various establishments. This activity of the Musée national has been going on for over ten years now. Since it started, during the 1983–84 school year, museum outreach workers have put together and made available to schools ten topics, four of which dealt with archaeology: (1) prehistory, (2) dating methods, (3) getting to know Mali through its historical and prehistoric sites, (4) Tellem history and culture.

This use of direct contact to inform those in charge of schools continued until the end of the 1988–89 school year. After four years of relations with school establishments, we were able to produce a booklet of activities to back up the contacts. It is entitled *Animation pédagogique* and sets out for those in charge of schools the range of activities that the Musée national can offer pupils and students at educational institutions. Initially five activities were offered: a general guided tour, a topical tour, an educational package, film shows and talks followed by discussions on one or a number of topics. Each year the document is corrected and updated in the light of criticisms and suggestions from those for whom it is designed, and also in the light of institutional difficulties. It is accompanied by a form of application for a tour that the teachers can submit to the museum's cultural and educational unit.

Seydou Ouattara

Figure 15.2 *Animation pédagogique*: a primary school class visiting the Musée National du Mali (*Photo: Cheik Oumar Keita, Musée National du Mali*)

Development of educational activities, 1983–93

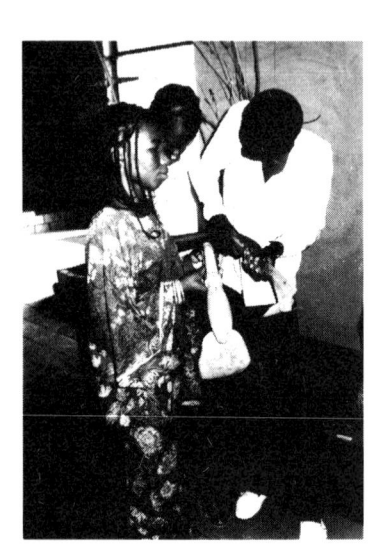

Figure 15.3 Blind pupils discovering objects by touch. (*Photo: Cheik Oumar Keita, Musée National du Mali*)

The school belonging to the Association malienne pour la promotion sociale des aveugles was the first to benefit from the educational support of the Musée national for teaching about archaeology. This educational activity consisted in dealing with the general topic while stressing its development in Mali, using the museum's collections: pebble tools, bifaces, touched-up shards, microliths, bone necklaces and tools, shells, etc. During the assessment that follows the activity, lapses of an educational nature were pointed out in the way the interaction with pupils was conducted and in the transmission of information by the outreach worker or educationalist.

The development of educational activities involving schools in the area of archaeology can be summarized as follows, on an academic year basis.

1983–84. As educational activity began when the school year was already well under way, the topic of archaeology was not much in demand, since it was dealt with in the earliest lessons of the teaching syllabus. The Association pour la promotion sociale des aveugles was the only school to request the topic. Consequently, during this trial year, only a few pupils took part in educational activities.

1984–85. This year the archaeological topics were adapted to the various levels of teaching, with a topic for the first cycle, one for the second cycle, one for technical and vocational general secondary education and one for higher education. A new activity was initiated for the understanding of prehistory: a tour with commentary on the prehistoric site of the grotto at Point G (Bamako). It was also during this year that the cultural and educational co-ordination unit received its first requests for visits.

1985–86. The Musée national's educational activity began with the exhibition 'Du Sahel au Sahara'. For this occasion a special document was prepared for the attention of educational institutions, setting out the theme and layout of the exhibition. The exhibition also gave the Musée national the opportunity to mount a large-scale information campaign aimed at the general public in the press and on radio and television on the archaeology of Mali. However, contacts with the heads of educational institutions were interrupted because of a trade union dispute between the administration and officials of the Ministry of Sport, Arts and Culture. The museum's cultural and educational outreach unit nevertheless met numerous requests for visits from educational establishments.

1986–87. A decline in the number of participants in educational activities was due to the continuance of the union dispute. But, in preparation for the school year, a draft booklet, *Activités Pédagogiques*, was planned and approved but could not be brought out. It was therefore not possible to make contacts with the school institutions in time. Nevertheless, two audio-visual documents on archaeology were added to the list of activities on offer: *Du Sahel au Sahara* (an interactive video-text programme) and *La Vie au Sahara* (a slide programme intended for 3–7 year olds).

1987–88. The acquisition of audio-visual equipment made it possible to offer other educational activities. The *Activités pédagogiques* guide was updated again. The clarifications and corrections arising from contacts with teachers made it possible to increase participation in archaeology-related educational programmes. It should be noted that Islamic establishments showed interest in the programmes.

1988–89. The *Activités pédagogiques* catalogue was replaced by a three-sheet pamphlet, *Animation Pédagogique*. The print run was exhausted in contacts with teachers. This new document with its various archaeological topics stimulated a substantial increase in the number participating in educational activities.

1989–90. Distribution of the *Animation Pédagogique* pamphlet made the schools in Bamako and the neighbouring districts more aware of the museum. From the very beginning of the 1990–91 school year numerous requests for educational activities were received from education committees and teachers. Contact was also made with new educational establishments. The Ministry lent its support by making its van available to the Educational Unit for transporting pupils from establishments situated a long way from the museum. The management of the museum did the same with its all-weather vehicle.

1990–91. The pamphlet on educational co-ordination was improved, developed and distributed to schools. But the political crisis that led to the overthrow of the old regime, and in particular the school strikes which accompanied it, seriously upset the running of educational activities. Although a few requests were met, activity fell back to the level of the 1987–88 school year.

1991–92. The school year was seriously disrupted by demonstrations. Educational establishments in Bamako underwent profound administrative change. Despite these disruptions, numerous requests were met, which increased the level of participation in archaeology-related educational activities.

1992–93. The school strikes continued. Nevertheless the number of participants in archaeology-related educational programmes rose slightly.

Figure 15.4 Terracotta tortoise from Bougouni region (*Photo: Musée National du Mali*)

Impact of the Musée national's educational activities

The Musée national's educational contribution to raising people's awareness of archaeology is highly rated by teachers and pupils. Pupils often come back to the museum with their school friends or even their parents to get to know more about archaeology or to seek out information about the activities in which they have taken part. In fact, today, for many teachers, the Musée national has become an educational aid of the greatest importance, particularly to illustrate their prehistory lessons. Its help is sought by school establishments, often quite independently of contacts with outreach workers. Some teachers have even sought the museum's educational support at the suggestion of their pupils.

Thanks to its archaeological exhibitions it has also become for many pupils and students a place to seek out their cultural identity and discover their culture, often an emotional, indeed passionate experience.

Moreover, recognition of the role the Musée national plays in the understanding and educational illustration of certain aspects of teaching programmes led to its being spared and indeed protected during disturbances organized by the Association des Élèves et Étudiants du Mali (AEEM).

Gaps and problems

The future of the Musée national's involvement in teaching programmes faces several difficulties.

Training. It is vital for the educators of the Musée national to upgrade their skills through appropriate training in archaeology and museum education programmes. In the last ten years we have been using the same methods and concepts in activities aimed at the school audience. Training would make it possible to fill the gaps that we detect in our team of programmers and make them more attractive.

Figure 15.5. Excavation of a burial site, Markala (*Photo: Musée National du Mali*)

Shortage of transport. Given the weakness of the urban transport network, the museum needs logistics that would enable it to transport pupils from remote establishments, and would enable outreach workers to ensure contact and follow-up with teachers.

Inadequacy of audio-visual equipment. The acquisition by the cultural and educational co-ordination unit of higher-performance and more manageable audio-visual equipment will make it possible to increase activities aimed at schools and make them more mobile.

Need for critical assessment. After ten years' experience the cultural and educational outreach unit feels the need for a critical appraisal of its activities. The sole critical analysis goes back to 1984–85 and concerned the adaptation of the topic of prehistory to the various cycles of education. To fill the conceptual gaps, since the 1990–91 school year the co-ordinators have taken the initiative of involving the head of the documentation and research section, a specialist in prehistory, in some of their school services.

In addition to these difficulties there are administrative ones, associated in particular with the salaries and allowances of the museum's educational outreach workers.

Some prospects

In order to support public education and help make the various aspects of Malian culture available to all sectors of society, the cultural and educational co-ordination unit conceived and submitted to the management a proposal for 'Caravanes découvertes culturelles du Mali' for pupils aged 13–14. The caravan is a journey of discovery, spread over one to three weeks, to enable pupils to become acquainted with some of the country's historic and prehistoric sites. The aim is to:

Seydou Ouattara

Figure 15.6 (*left*)   Terracotta statuette, Thial, Ténenkou (*Photo: Musée National du Mali*)

Figure 15.7 (*right*)   Terracotta head from Jenné (*Photo: Musée National du Mali*)

Figure 15.8 (*left*)   Terracotta bedpost from Macina (*Photo: Musée National du Mali*)

Figure 15.9 (*right*)   Terracotta statuette from Fakola (*Photo: Musée National du Mali*)

1. Make young pupils more aware of the national cultural heritage so as to develop in them greater awareness of its wealth and its problems.

2. Give new impetus to the museum's work.

Since the 1986–87 school year the Musée national has been engaged in intensive activity aimed at persuading those in charge of education to integrate the educational activities of the Musée national and the study of the national culture in school syllabuses. The prospects are encouraging for the coming years, and already the cultural and educational outreach unit has been invited to participate in a national meeting to draw up the official syllabuses of history and geography in basic education.

At the same time the outreach workers of the Musée national are endeavouring to develop co-operative and exchange relations with the archaeologists of the Institut des sciences humaines.

Finally we hope to develop archaeological exchanges with the educational departments of museums in our sub-region and, eventually, to enable them to benefit from our experience of developing programmes for opening the museum to schools.

16 Côte d'Ivoire
The Value of the Remains of Material Culture to the Knowledge of the Peoples

GILBERT GONNIN

Ecole normale supérieure, Abidjan

Professor Jean Devisse wrote in 1981, 'An historian who is deprived of archaeology in Africa is blind and deaf to the heart of the past of that continent; an archaeologist who loses sight of the objectives of the historian soon ceases to be in contact with the "demand for history" of the peoples of Africa. And we must not forget that it is those peoples who are the especial recipients of the discovery of their past . . .' (Devisse, 1981: 5). It no longer needs to be demonstrated that archaeological evidence, 'remains of human activities that give a concrete view of the past' (Salmon, 1986), is vital for knowledge of peoples and their history. In Côte d'Ivoire, although there is little in the way of research projects because of the lack of resources, archaeology has continued to develop over the last few decades. Nevertheless access by the general public and even by researchers from neighbouring disciplines to the results of its work remains a problem.

As for museums, places for the conservation of objects enshrining cultural identity and archaeological remains, they are not always seen, either by citizens or even by some researchers, as repositories of a history. Despite the efforts to promote them, they still appear as 'enclosed areas' reserved to a minority of initiates, which creates a problem of communication, and communication is a condition of all exploitation. Thus, instead of enabling people to know one another and explain their history to one another, the material products of civilization – whether of archaeological or other origin – seem to have but little relevance to current culture. It is therefore justifiable to ask how archaeological evidence and museum collections can be of any use to citizens asking questions about the long-term evolution of their cultures. How can they, or the museums themselves as places for preservation and conservation, intervene in the dissemination of that culture?

Seen thus, it is important, on the basis of experience of teaching and of preparing school textbooks and works of popularization, to draw up a balance sheet of the use of the results of archaeological research and museum collections for reconstructing and disseminating the history and culture of the peoples of Côte d'Ivoire. The observations will serve as a basis for thinking about the prospects of a better understanding and greater use of those cultures by the descendants of those who built them.

The material products of culture as teaching aids

Museum collections

Of the four conventional functions of a museum we shall focus particularly on that which enables it to act as a 'data bank' or 'source of information and knowledge' (Rose, 1988): communicating or presenting collections to a wide and varied public so as to make the direct use of the resources of the museum possible for educational purposes. As Alexander Spoehi, the former director of the Bishop Museum in Hawaii, says, 'no museum can be content to be a store and collections that no one sees are useless. The objects held in museums must not only be brought together, identified and studied but also put on display and published' (Rose, 1988: 43). Have museums in Côte d'Ivoire fully played their educational and scientific role?

There are two sorts of museum in Côte d'Ivoire: public museums (the Musée national in Abidjan and the regional museums) and private museums. The collections of the former, like those of the National Museum in Abidjan, were 'largely built up during the colonial period. They are not representative of the country's material culture and suffer from the absence of the proper documentation' (Savané, 1991: 1). As for the private museums, notably those built up by members of new religions, such as the one at Vavoua, their collections are regarded either as the work of Satan (by the devotees of the new religion), and thus of no interest, while being feared, or as expressing the rejection of cultural identity. In both cases the problems of interest and communication are posed, and only if they are resolved can their collections be used as an educational instrument.

Authors of school textbooks and popular works on history and culture make little use of the collections of the museums of Côte d'Ivoire. While they are sometimes resorted to, to illustrate their works, authors generally prefer personal collections or the collections of other institutions.

Thus in Jean Noël Loucou's *Histoire de la Côte d'Ivoire*, of twenty-four photographic illustrations, five are from the collections of the Institut d'histoire d'art et d'archéologie africains, fifteen are from the works of Holas, Tauxier, Behrens, etc., but none is from a museum in Côte d'Ivoire.

Similarly, in the *Manuel d'histoire des cours élémentaires*, none of the 159 illustrations comes from museums in Côte d'Ivoire, or at least none is identified as such. But in fact twenty come from the Ministry of Cultural Affairs and five from Photoivoire.

In the *Manuel d'histoire des cours moyens*, of 209 illustrations only two are from the Musée national in Abidjan, while twelve are from the Musée de l'homme and three from Tegdaoust archaeological expeditions.

The *Manuel d'histoire de la Côte d'Ivoire* of the first cycle of secondary education (edited by Pierre Kipre) includes not a single illustration from museums in Côte d'Ivoire, either. The editors have mainly used illustrations from the *Mémorial de Côte d'Ivoire*, whose illustrations, where they do come from Ivoirien sources, are from personal collections, the Bibliothèque nationale, *Fraternité-Matin* and Photo-Info.

It can be seen that the editors of these books did not make the best use of museums in Côte d'Ivoire. It is self-evident that users of these educational tools, who will be the citizens of tomorrow, will continue to regard museums as the cemetery of material cultures.

Nevertheless it must be stressed that, to make the public more aware of its collections and new discoveries, the Musée national in Abidjan has stepped up the number of exhibitions showing the works of sculptors at the Abidjan museum (1987 and 1988), the treasures of the communes of Bingerville, Divo and Bondoukou (1989), the exhibition 'Restaurer et préserver' (1990), exhibitions on the stones from Gohitafla. Yet, given the absence of proper documentation, exhibitions of ancient items cannot satisfy the public. Nor has it been possible to estimate the real audience for these exhibitions.

The data of archaeology

Although relatively young, Ivoirien archaeology made remarkable progress in the 1980s, developing knowledge of the history and material cultures of the peoples of the country. The problem that arises is not only how to extract from the archaeological data information on the history and culture of the peoples of Côte d'Ivoire but also how to disseminate the results of research. What conclusions can be drawn from existing works and textbooks?

Thanks to its discoveries, archaeology makes it possible to assert that Côte d'Ivoire was never empty of people, and that the process of settlement extends at least from late Stone Age times to the first millennium AD. 'Although there are few archaeological sites in Côte d'Ivoire, there are nevertheless some indications that enable us to conclude that most regions of the country were settled in prehistoric times' (Diabaté, 1983). Major old Stone Age sites have been located with the discovery of large amounts of material (pebble tools, bifaces, picks, racloirs and grattoirs). Late Stone Age material is to be found almost everywhere, evidenced either by quartz tools which folk belief regards as stones produced by thunder, or by large quantities of pottery and large shell middens along the lagoons.

This reminder of archaeological discoveries is intended to underline the role of archaeology in the establishment of the chronology of human presence on the territory of Côte d'Ivoire and the relation between archaeology and history. The problem of the use of archaeology by specialists in allied disciplines is still there: what is the functional value of archaeological remains? What place do they occupy in existing works and educational textbooks?

The iconography constructed from archaeological discoveries takes up little space in the illustrations of educational materials. It is not the sort of thing that will develop the interest of those being taught, particularly the youngest, in prehistory and ancient history, or familiarize them with the remains that reflect the cultural ingenuity of various periods, from the old Stone Age down to modern times. Illustrations make it possible to reconcile two educational objectives: developing knowledge and know-how by making knowledge less theoretical and more practical.

In addition the books do not sufficiently show the specificity of archaeology and its role in our knowledge of peoples' history. The whole effect is to make it look as though the results of archaeological research are simply being pirated.

Finally, despite the advances achieved, the uncertainties of archaeology, notably the as yet unconfirmed dating hypotheses, make it difficult to use archaeological data in textbooks, which are educational tools intended for non-specialists in archaeology (teachers, parents and pupils). In such works there is no room for on-going debate.

In sum, despite all the contributions of archaeology and, to a lesser extent, museums to knowledge of the history and culture of the peoples of Côte d'Ivoire, very little use is made of material objects and the fruits of archaeological research to teach and disseminate that culture. Can we look forward to better use being made of them for teaching purposes?

The use of material remains as educational aids

The curator of the Musée national rightly describes his establishment as an 'educational tool at the service of Ivoirien researchers, teachers, artists, scholars, students and citizens' (Savané and Pautonnier, 1989). A noble mission that the museums of Côte d'Ivoire do not as yet fully fulfil. What then must be done to achieve this aspiration?

Enhancing the standing of museums through a range of educational methods

Users of museums and their collections constitute a diverse public. For that reason there is a need to attract and even seduce visitors, and to educate them by interesting them, which involves both the museum personnel and the way objects are presented.

Better use of museum collections also involves closer collaboration between the museums and the educational system. In any event, a more proactive policy towards schools as institutions is called for: information, group visits, the creation of an educational department, exhibitions for children are the only ways of ensuring 'dissemination of the heritage among young people' (Savané, 1991).

Finally, illustrations in books and school textbooks need to be given a dual educational value: they must be illustrated, but they should be more informative about the sources of the illustrations. More particularly, especially in books designed for the lower classes, it is essential to change the position of credit lines acknowledging the source of photographs. Rather than being in small print at the end of the book they should appear under each illustration, so indicating the conservation role of some institutions, including museums. In addition, publications on museums, currently noticeable by their absence, can also be useful to teachers, as they can also be to the department responsible for producing teaching material in the Ministry of National Education.

Making archaeological data more widely known

Archaeological discoveries have the potential to be used in education, as they can be used to give a concrete aspect to teaching in several disciplines (history, architecture, crafts, etc.). In addition, archaeological discoveries can make it possible to save or give new life to some forms of production, especially artistic and architectural ones. But if it is to happen the information must be circulated, first among archaeologists themselves, then between them and specialists in other disciplines. But, as the guide to the exhibition 'L'histoire de la Côte d'Ivoire vue par l'archéologie' stresses, archaeologists keep their work secret, often alleging that a thesis is being written. In fact even when the scholarly work is completed the results remain inaccessible.[1]

Although archaeology is a discipline taught by specialists, its results are widely used by educationalists in related disciplines. It is thus important for the latter to learn something about the science whose discoveries they are using. Good collaboration is needed between archaeologists and researchers in other disciplines, not just at the stage of interpretation but from the excavation onward, that is, from the point when the archaeologist begins to turn the pages of his book of 'travel through material culture'.

Conclusion

Material remains make an important and permanent contribution to knowledge of the peoples of Côte d'Ivoire: historical knowledge, knowledge of the transformations that man has wrought on his environment, knowledge of the cultural diversity and complementarity of Ivoirien heritages. Yet ways must be sought to ensure that these material remains of lost culture are better known and exploited, since they constitute 'the sum of experiences accumulated by generations in many key areas' (Johanson and Edey, 1990: 194). No one has the right to ignore them, and no one has the right to a monopoly of them.

Note

1. See the collective volume *L'Histoire de la Côte d'Ivoire vue par l'archéologie* (Abidjan, 1993).

References

Devisse, J. 1981. 'La recherche en archéologie et sa contribution à l'histoire de l'Afrique', *Recherche, pédagogie et culture* (Paris) IX, 55.

Diabaté, H. (ed.). 1983. *Mémorial de Côte d'Ivoire*. Abidjan.

Johanson, Donald C. and Edey, M. 1990. *Lucy: the beginnings of humankind*. London: Penguin.

Rose, R. G. 1988. 'Les technologies de l'information et de la communication au musée: la démarche suédoise', *Museum* 160.

Salmon, P. 1986. *Introduction à l'histoire de l'Afrique*. Brussels: Hayez.

Savané, Y. 1991. *Musée national d'Abidjan. Bilan d'activités 1986–90. Perspectives pour les prochaines années*. Abidjan: Musée national.

Savané, Y. and Pautonnier, E. 1989. *Musée national d'Abidjan*. Abidjan: Musée national.

17 Benin
Museums & Education

RASHIDA AYARI DE SOUZA
Direction du patrimoine culturel, Cotonou

The museum in Africa must be a welcoming and friendly place, an instrument of education through objects as a means of communication and as a subject of discourse, a medium of integrated topics. It must be open to interdisciplinary collaboration and to ever more varied partnerships. It is a place above all for the spoken word, for dialogue among visitors, professionals and researchers through educational, promotional and cultural activities that provoke questions and arouse debate, criticism and the clash of ideas, while making people aware of new information and thinking about the past. This dialogue must rest on active museum teaching which consists in presenting knowledge and facilitating understanding of the world through clear and simple ideas.

Introduction

The museum sees itself as a means of educating its community. However, the variety and contradictory nature of society's expectations means that this educational role involves several strategies if it is to be implemented.
 1. Cultural information and its dissemination about the current state of knowledge.
 2. Scientific popularization.
 3. Training.
The museum must also help the public to adapt and become aware of the socio-economic conditions of the environment, which are in constant flux.
Scientific and technical culture is an essential component of culture in general. African societies live downstream from and on the periphery of fallout from technological changes in post-industrial societies and cannot enclose themselves in outdated learning. That culture is today seen as operational knowledge, since, beyond an interest in science, it makes it possible to construct a new national identity rooted in history, but also seen in scientific achievements and better knowledge of the national endeavour. It implies the democratization of learning, a sharing which makes scientific thought and results more accessible to the general public. The museum is one of the means of disseminating and communicating that learning, since:
 1. It enables people to see, through its exhibitions, by opening its doors and facilitating access to the general public.
 2. It enables people to know about, discover and acquire information.

Museums and education

Generally speaking, informal education has several aims:
1. To help towards a better understanding of the world.
2. To implement targeted and assessed teaching activities.
3. To establish relations of confidence and a communications-based approach.

Education helps us to understand the history, creations and problems of the world through the acquisition of scientific, aesthetic and historical knowledge. It provides codes for access to knowledge through the intellectual acquisition and comprehension of languages (languages in the plural: languages, symbols, objects, media, etc.).

It rests on a sequential organization of the objectives of training, since education means gradually leading and guiding towards an end, useful and positive knowledge, and includes objectives of mastery, transfer and expression. It involves the cognitive, affective and psycho-motive aspects of the human mind. It is based on a relationship of confidence between one who knows and one who does not know, since it ends up modifying attitudes, values and judgement. Education in the museum rests on:
1. Experimentation with reality through the object and space.
2. A capacity for analysis and synthesis.
3. Tolerance and a critical mind.

The museum must be one educational tool among others, capable of helping to forge intellectual autonomy through observation and creative imagination.

Today in Africa there is a growing demand for education, but often the formal systems cannot meet needs and expectations. Of course the museum cannot replace the school, which remains a highly structured institution, but, being more flexible and more open, it can respond with appropriate cultural products and complementary activities. It stands as an alternative reception centre, open unrestrictedly, since it owes its whole existence to its public, whose loyalty it endeavours to secure and which it endeavours to enlarge by developing a range of museum products. In this context a form of museum teaching develops which involves:
1. Exploiting the resources of communication.
2. The educational use of objects.
3. Diversifying responses according to the relevant public.

Why has the museum become a place of teaching and a convenient means of achieving the aims of awakening and promoting an approach that sensitizes people to education?

The museum is a place for questioning, thinking and synthesis whose communication strategies rest on a cross-cultural approach and on integrated topics. It seeks the integration of the various fields of research focused on the same end, mankind.

In our time fields of learning are more focused, but they have ceased to be watertight. In practice we are moving in the direction of the multi-disciplinarity, complementarity and interaction of different fields of learning. The museological approach takes more and more account of this multi-faceted collaboration. The museum is one of the tools that can promote the initiation and dissemination of knowledge among a range of publics, since:

Figure 17.1 Two anthropomorphous stone heads found by chance at Bidojato
(*Photo: Blaise Amegah*)

1. It has the means of display (objects, exhibitions, audio-visual equipment).
2. It is a place for communication and human contact where human relations are the chief resource.
3. It is a space for the exchange of ideas and experiences, which facilitates a dynamic approach through the spoken word. Through an open museology the museum makes it possible to speak out and criticize, and 'gives back the power of speech'.

The museum works through active teaching and a redefinition of roles, since it is not an extension of the hierarchical system of the school. The outreach worker is not a substitute for the teacher but a facilitator, a resource person who helps to teach people to look, by displaying or by discovering new dimensions of knowledge.

Museums and outreach in Benin

In Benin the national museums do not possess archaeological collections, although some sites where museums are established, such as Abomey, Porto Novo and Ouidah, have a significant potential. The introduction of archaeology into Beninois museums might open up new prospects of development and of exhibitions and educational co-ordination activities. Nevertheless, there is co-operation between the Department of Archaeology at the Université nationale du Bénin and the Directorate of Cultural Heritage in charge of national museums. In particular, joint research teams are being set up for a number of projects (for example, the Ouessé project, an inventory of monuments and sites).

Figure 17.2 The archaeological research team of the Université National de Bénin laying out the site of the excavation at Bidojato
(*Photo: Blaise Amegah*)

Figure 17.3 The start of an archaeological excavation
(*Photo: Blaise Amegah*)

Educational programmes

Educational programmes in Benin are peripheral activities of support for museums. The activities are structured at three levels:

1. School demand. It is significant. However, the responses vary considerably from museum to museum. Generally we organize guided tours, often of a general kind, at the request of schools. Sometimes our outreach workers meet requests for special tours, more targeted than thematic ones,

associated above all with the historical exploitation of the royal palaces, cultural and historic sites as well as with the collections of the historical museums in Abomey and Porto Novo/Honmè.

2. At the royal palace at Honmè, which is essentially a site museum, a particular effort has been made to introduce an educational presentation for the benefit of school groups during guided tours. A synoptic table has been issued of the history of the royal reigns and genealogies, for use by teachers, even on outside visits. This aid makes it possible to give children a sense of time and chronology through a concrete display. In this museum there is also a permanent workshop for children, run by two educators. It organizes manual activities with groups of schoolchildren (drawing, colouring, collage, painting and free creation activities) which in 1992 led to an exhibition of drawings by children on the environment.

3. For students at the Université nationale du Bénin we often organize thematic tours, mainly technical ones, in association with the teachers, including an introduction to the management of the collection and the cultural heritage in general.

In February 1993 the Heritage Directorate, in partnership with a non-governmental organization, the Centre d'activités éducatives du Bénin, ran a week-long training course at the Musée Honmè (Porto Novo) for primary school teachers to initiate them into use of the museum as a medium and an educational instrument.

Cultural outreach

For the general public we offer guided tours, adapting the content of each tour to the visitors – nationals, intellectuals, tourists. In this type of presentation we often use the national language (often the two dominant languages of the region), the guides being trained to do so. The tours are conducted upon request in French, English or a national language.

The national museums also welcome festivals, artistic displays and a variety of ceremonies. They are gradually becoming cultural spaces for meetings, exchanges and artistic expression. Thus:

1. Every year Abomey opens its doors to the great royal ceremonies in November, December and January.

2. Honmè/Porto Novo welcomed the African theatre festival 'Afrique de demain' in 1993.

3. Ouidah witnessed a great artistic outpouring during the 'Ouidah-92/Retrouvailles Afrique-Amérique' festival in February 1993.

Communication and publics

Faced with an ever more diverse clientele (pupils, illiterate children, intellectuals, tourists, etc.), we are attempting to readjust our priorities by paying special heed to the publics represented by young people and the general public, by adopting an approach that is more educational than document-focused. To that end we are moving towards:

1. Rethinking the arrangement of the museums to develop new ways of communicating with our visitors.

Figure 17.4a (*left*) Student from the Université Nationale du Bénin carrying out an archaeological excavation (*Photo: Blaise Amegah*)

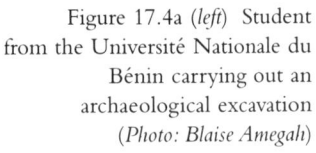

Figure 17.4b (*right*) Checking the stratigraphy of an excavation (*Photo: Blaise Amegah*)

2. Replacing classified displays with a more synthesising presentation that popularizes knowledge through an anthropological view of culture, involving a multidisciplinary approach which reflects a scientific and social need for the museum.

3. Involving research so as to use our collections and historical spaces to present knowledge and learning that are less disjointed and less compartmentalized, to transmit basic, coherent information through a synthesis of scientific approaches.

Generally, to give the museums greater credibility and make them less boring and conventional, we need to restructure our displays and build new presentations which do not convey a picture of a culture or of learning that stresses simply the leisure aspect (in the sense of a mere discovery of an unknown or exotic area) but makes it as real as possible so as to grab the visitor's attention and lead him to learn something and acquire information. That is an educational commitment which transforms the institution into an educational instrument, entailing many demands:

1. More complex, meaningful and representative exhibitions that stand out by selection that wins attention and reveals information by splitting messages up, simplifying them and making them appropriate to the target public.

2. A programme of structured co-ordination that includes specific objectives, the identification of target publics, topics more responsive to what the public wants, a definite budget, a strict time scale for work, qualitative and quantitative assessment and ready communication with the public, notably through its use of a variety of languages.

3. Effective outreach staff. Oral communication is an essential dimension for our publics, since it makes possible a dynamic approach to speech

Figure 17.5a and b Anthropological survey of pottery of the Ouessé region (*Photo: Blaise Amegah*)

(exchanges, talks, literacy, oral traditions, etc.), rapid assimilation and response, a sense of contact and a spirit of togetherness such as to establish a climate of listening and openness.

This new orientation stimulates learning in two directions:

1. For our publics: discovery, the acquisition of knowledge and better circulation of information.
2. For museum professionals: experiential learning, 'on the job' and informally.

In Africa the museum lives from its visitors. However, visitors ought also to find a climate of availability and choice in museums, without being subject to rigid directed tours or never-ending explanations cut off from their living environment.

The publics of children and young people are trying out a sensorial appropriation of knowledge (an aesthetic of forms, colours, speech, etc.), and that discovery, that pleasuring of the senses, is developing in them an affective memory that can be strengthened by gradually awakening, through curiosity and imagination, a taste for scientific research.

Today we are required to promote the imperative of the 'democracy of knowledge' (cognitive democracy), since learning cannot remain the monopoly of a minority of 'experts' or a scientific community reduced to isolation.

Through educational action to popularize and inform in the museum we can make a contribution to overcoming the problems of the community (poverty, waste of resources, violation of human rights, illiteracy, etc.). The museum is not a panacea, or a place for hoarding knowledge, but a space for speech where various and complementary languages can be used to reflect on social realities and promote 'cognitive democracy'.

Figure 17.6 (*left*) Pots and potter's tools: scrapers/rakes and rollers for decorating pots, Ouessé (*Photo: Blaise Amegah*)

Figure 17.7 (*right*) A potter completing her pots (*Photo: Blaise Amegah*)

Figure 17.8 Sale of pots in the market at Ouessé (*Photo: Blaise Amegah*)

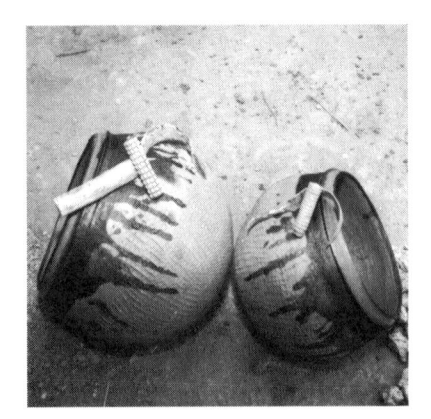

Conclusion The museum exists through its publics. We are often criticized for being lethargic or living in a sort of priestly isolation and neglecting our publics. We expect them to come to us of their own accord. The fact is that those publics are our best allies, the living evidence of our effectiveness and the educational and cultural impact of our services. Only a minority of nationals visit Benin's museums, while the cities are abundant reservoirs of potential visitors. Our essential challenge is: how to open and facilitate access to this general public, how to create effective conditions for receiving them and above all how to present cultural and scientific products that really arouse their interest and induce them to visit the museums?

Today, in Africa, museums have acquired professional knowledge and have teams which, through their integrated and multidisciplinary services, can act as a catalyst to increase visiting of their institutions and attract new publics by reorienting their exhibitions towards more educational, more 'consciousness-raising' topics, closer to the actual problems people experience, and by increasing the number of cultural displays. African museums are gradually becoming social instruments. Our role is to make these institutions more permeable to the social fabric through the dissemination, education and popularization of scientific work and research. Such popularization must be conducted in national languages, while avoiding confusion and reductive simplification.

Our chief objective is to fertilize the activity of museums by becoming cross-disciplinary, getting involved in related activities in partnership and transforming museums into social, friendly spaces for communicating and circulating knowledge in the community.

18 Cameroon
The Teaching & Transmission of Archaeology in a National Museum

GERMAIN LOUMPET
Commission for setting up the Museum of Cameroon, Yaoundé

As with all the scientific disciplines in the Museum of Cameroon, the main purpose of archaeology is educational. Research, education and communication become correlative notions in a general process whose importance lies precisely in the definition of a paradigm of interactions and feedback between the medium and the publics. This approach justifies the development of a theoretical and experimental programme for the acquisition and selection of empirical knowledge and know-how intended to sustain transmission and participation strategies.

Archaeological research in Cameroon

A survey of the state of archaeological research in Cameroon is appropriate here to help bring out the full importance and scope of the museum's scientific programme.

Archaeology in Cameroon is still at the stage of surveys. Research remains scattered, fragmentary and, in general, confined to the Sudano-Sahelian savanna regions, which are undeniably easier of access. The whole equatorial forest area has long remained unexplored. These gaps mean that we have only a partial picture of the general framework of the successive cultures of Cameroon and provide even less of a basis for objective delineation of presumed cultural areas or settlement centres.

Carved stone objects or other remains were often picked up around the country from the 1920s onwards by colonial expeditions, in particular by geographers, geologists and ethnologists. It is difficult to locate the sites today because they were poorly identified. The only publications relating to archaeology dating from that time amount to no more than mere notes or mentions in administrative reports. In 1965 a new era began for Cameroonian archaeology, marked by systematic investigations. But these efforts remained concentrated in the north of the country.

In this context, J. Hervieu (1970) drew up an outline of the palaeoclimatic evolution of northern Cameroon, along with a classification of the historical cultures associated with it. Alain Marliac carried out systematic surveys, with the aim of identifying the location of certain sites. He studied the rock art site at Bidzar and drew up an archaeological map of northern Cameroon (1973).

Other researchers made a not insignificant contribution to knowledge of the archaeology of northern Cameroon: N. David (1971) uncovered man-

Figure 18.1 Northeast façade of the Museum of Cameroun, Yaoundé

made mounds on the Benue and Mayo Kedi, notably at Nassarao II; Jean-Paul and Annie Lebeuf (1969, 1977) carried out excavations in the Sao area and published an archaeological map of the region around Lake Chad.

The vast forest area in the south has clearly aroused less enthusiasm on the part of archaeologists, and systematic research there began only in the early 1980s. A few surface remains were reported (E. Mveng, 1968), but they were not subject to closer study.

From 1980 to 1983 the Belgian archaeologist Pierre de Maret undertook excavations at Obobogo, near Yaoundé, where he uncovered a sequence of two occupations, one dated to 6000 BC and the other to the fourth century BC. Ditch sites were discovered at Ndindan, Okolo and Nkometu dating from the sixth to the third centuries BC. The site at Oliga, discovered by Jacques Montallet and excavated by J. M. Essomba (1992), contains an ancient furnace whose slag is dated to 2800–1800 BC.

Since 1985 Alexandra and Germain Loumpet have been carrying out systematic research in eastern Cameroon, near Batouri, where they have discovered a group of prehistoric sites, the largest of which, at Biti, has yielded abundant Acheulian-made stone tools. The sites at Béké and Timangoro appear to be even older. Several concentrations of caves and rock shelters have also been uncovered by the same archaeologists in the neighbourhood of Mbalmayo and are evidence of sequences of occupation of which the most recent at least are contemporaneous with the Iron Age.

The sites in the north-west of the country are similarly evidence of the presence of man by the end of the late Pleistocene era, mainly in the shelters at Mbi, Shum Laka and Abeke. This work makes it possible to outline a pattern of evolution that puts the oldest known aspects of the peopling of

Figure 18.2 Excavations at Sao (Mission Lebeuf, 1983)

Cameroon almost a million years ago and opens up important avenues for research in the Quaternary period and the origins of man and his cultural development all through the Pleistocene period.

In addition, because it extends over many degrees of latitude, Cameroon has a great variety of natural environments, a fact which favours an approach using specific models of adaptation and evolutionary patterns in relation to the different eco-systems over the ages.

Despite this significant potential, the lack of an archaeology policy in Cameroon today – which would involve establishing a programme and structures for the study and publication of the results – is to be deplored. Such a situation does not encourage the circulation of scientific information among the various publics and makes it impossible to assess the importance of discoveries and their consequences.

Only the university offers teaching in archaeology, within the framework of a supplementary option in the history course, but it still does not offer specialization in training as an archaeologist. The museum stands as the sole instrument that can currently raise awareness and act as an essential intermediary between the public and archaeological research.

The archaeology programme of the museum

The overall plan for the layout of the space assigned to the museum allocates semi-permanent exhibition halls and a research office to archaeology, together with all the museum's technical infrastructure for study, dissemination and popularization.

The Museum of Cameroon's scientific programme outlines an itinerary which seeks to be educational, following a synchronic pattern that is not

Figure 18.3 (*left*) Stone tools from Biti

Figure 18.4 (*right*) The shaft at the prehistoric site at Biti

exclusively linear, within which archaeology occupies an essential position and starts the sequence after the presentation of the natural environments and the periodized contexts of ecology.

This importance attributed to archaeology rests on two kinds of argument: (1) an ideological one, as the historical foundation of rootedness in time and space; and (2) a scientific one, as a major asset in knowledge of the physiological evolution of man and cultural ethnogenesis. Finally, archaeology is a vital source for the history of peoples with an oral tradition.

Exhibitions

The formula of semi-permanent exhibitions makes for a great degree of flexibility in the choice of topics and the way they are handled. Varied approaches to a given problem can thus be offered, in order to encourage debate and participation.

The organization of the archaeological spaces of the museum rests on a distribution which, while following the broad chronological and cultural divisions of the history of mankind, remains nevertheless fundamentally arbitrary in its form. In such an approach prehistoric archaeology simply provides modular benchmarks within which sequences and context are introduced which aim to convey sets of facts whose mechanisms will be sought out and patterns suggested.

Every archaeological exhibition will have to encompass the following features in the way it is put together:

1. *Chronology.* In an anthropological approach, it represents a goal only to the extent that it brings out a dynamic whose continuity it is possible to grasp.

Figure 18.5 (*top, left*) Site where the axes and flints were found

Figure 18.6 (*top, right*) 11 metres down

Figure 18.7 (*right*) Water had to be pumped out

2. *Ecology*. The environment regarded as a cause brings in all the transformations of the system and hence of technology, demography or the economy. Establishing the universal impact of this principle is difficult, but it functions at least operationally in analysis of the independent variables of global culture.

Figure 18.8 Rock shelter at Nda Akoa II

3. *Cultural technology.* The study of cultural technology seeks to establish the relationship between techniques and other social phenomena and stresses the interdependence of the elements that make up the system.

There are three levels of approach:
1. Objects, the results of actions on matter.
2. Processes, which make up operational linkages.
3. Empirical knowledge.

The level of communication and education

The pattern of the museum–public–research linkage of the Museum of Cameroon applies to archaeology generally and involves a three-dimensional structure of organization, content and mediation.

1. *Organization* constitutes the ideological armature regulating the whole process. It is represented by the museum's organization chart.
2. *Content* is the result, *a posteriori,* of a quest for meaning and signification.
3. *Mediation* attempts to achieve a correlation between meaning, signification, cognition and feedback.

The communication project designed to promote communication of and education about archaeology in the museum takes into account the very nature and object of this knowledge.

On the one hand, archaeology stands as a scholarly science and thus as one which the general public knows little of or simply ignores. On the other, the epistemological breach with history remains fluid, and archaeology then appears as a method or a discipline auxiliary to history, occurring as such in curricula as a supplement to the university course. Finally, archaeology retains

Figure 18.9 Close-up of rock shelter at Nda Akoa II

the image of a mysterious and spectacular science devoted to great discoveries of impressive and remote civilizations, which further adds to the feeling of remoteness and strangeness. Any communication strategy will have above all to attempt a *rapprochement* between archaeology and the public, through familiarization, in order to arouse interest in the work methods, objectives and limits of this science and finally the value of its content.

In order to make the content accord with the message, action would seem to need to be directed as a priority towards:

1. Identifying the publics through a breakdown by such categories as age, sex, level of education, socio-professional status, etc.
2. Assessing average rates and patterns of attendance.
3. Defining the various hourly peaks.

The information will make it possible to plan programmes of exhibitions and visits targeted at a specific public, or set of publics. The quest for interaction between public and archaeology will also have to be based on the mounting of exhibitions. Archaeology offers the advantage of using an essentially material support to justify its method of investigation, which facilitates the construction of displays from remains and thus provides an initiation to a mode of apprehending scientific discourse and scenarios, and gives access to empirical knowledge. In the same way, the visual aspects must be exploited through the introduction of an iconographical system based on simple patterns, colours and photographs as well as comparisons.

Finally the archaeological outreach of the museum is jointly entrusted to the museum's educators and archaeologists, who have to conceive the means of achieving the greatest possible involvement of the public. The practical options are:

1. Looking for possible interaction between conventional teaching programmes, for the school and university publics, and an informal system put together for the purpose by the museum's experts.
2. Implementing programmes of visits in the various local languages, on a rolling basis.
3. Putting together travelling exhibitions directed at the rural areas.
4. Organizing workshops for practical initiation into the techniques of archaeology through reconstructions built either in an exhibition or within the museum.
5. The simultaneous use of publicly owned documentary and audio-visual equipment to back the exhibitions up.

References

David, N. 1971. 'Recherches archéologiques dans la vallée de la Bénoué', *Revue camerounaise d'histoire* 1, 212–96.
Essomba, J. M. 1992. *Civilisation du fer et sociétés en Afrique centrale: le cas du Cameroun.* Collection Racines du présent, Paris: l'Harmattan.
Hervieu, J. 1970. 'Contribution à l'étude des industries lithiques du Nord Cameroun: mise au point et données nouvelles', *Cahiers de l'ORSTOM,* Sciences humaines VIII (3), 1–40.
Lebeuf, J. P. 1969. *Carte archéologique des abords du lac Tchad.* Paris: CNRS.
Lebeuf, J. P. and A. 1977. *Les Arts des Sao.* Paris: du Chêne.
Loumpet, G. 1987. 'Eléments de synthèse pour un cadre paléoclimatique et paléoécologique quaternaire au Cameroun: première approche d'une industrie lithique ancienne dans les dépôts alluviaux de Biti en Haute-Sangha, Est-Cameroun/Ouest RCA'. Ph.D. thesis, Université de Paris I.
—— 1991. 'La philosophie du Musée du Cameroun', in G. Loumpet and A. Loumpet-Galitzine, *Le Projet du Musée du Cameroun* 1, *Présentation des études.* Yaoundé: Ministère de l'information et de la culture.
—— 1992a. 'Environnement, anthropogenèse et culture: le paradoxe d'une interaction rétroactive', *Actes du Colloque sur l'environnement.* Yaoundé: Ecole polytechnique.
—— 1992b. 'Les hommes préhistoriques du Cameroun méridional forestier', *Terroirs* 1, 20–6. Yaoundé: Gerdés.
—— 1995. 'Musée et idéologie nationale', *Culture-Info* (Yaoundé) 1, 12–13.
Loumpet, G. and Loumpet-Galitzine, A. 1992. *Le Projet du Musée du Cameroun* II, *Transformation de l'ancien palais présidentiel en Musée national.* Yaoundé: Ministère de l'information et de la culture.
Marliac, A. 1973. 'Prospections archéologiques au Cameroun', *Cahiers de l'ORSTOM,* Sciences humaines X, 47–114.
Mveng, E. 1968. 'Archéologie camerounaise: découverte des poteries de Mimetala', *Bulletin française pour les recherches et études camerounaises* T3.
—— 1971. 'Archéologie camerounaise: Mvolyé', *Revue camerounaise d'histoire* 1, 123–7.

19 Kenya
Museums, Archaeology & the Public

GEORGE H. O. ABUNGU
National Museums of Kenya, Mombasa

Museums, archaeology and the public is a subject of increasing interest, especially in developing countries, where the concepts of museums and archaeology have for long been beyond the domain of the majority of the population. Museums have been viewed by many as places for the display of cultural materials which are visited only by a particular group of people – in most cases, tourists and school parties. To some a museum is a place where 'dead' items are kept and preserved. To some the picture that comes to mind is of a gallery full of exhibits of old cultural artefacts and other related material; to others it is a research and an educational institution.

In Kenya a large percentage of the population can today claim to have visited the National Museums of Kenya during early childhood, a time when they could not actually appreciate the significance of the vast collection of items exhibited, or the other activities going on in the museum. The subject of museums, archaeology and the public therefore becomes of particular interest not only to the archaeologists or museologists but also to African or Third World governments. Questions such as 'Does "museum" mean the same thing in Africa as in Europe or America?' 'Is it possible to speak of an African museum?' are now becoming significant. In Kenya the question 'What is a museum?' is one which lingers in most people's minds and cannot be answered in one simple sentence, as can be seen from the above notions.

Archaeology, on the other hand, has remained a subject for a select few, despite the fact that it has been practised in Africa since at least the early years of this century. This state of affairs has ruled despite the fact that East Africa has produced the earliest evidence of human origins and possesses some of the richest archaeological and palaeontological deposits.

Despite the lack of understanding of muscum activities, and the fact that archaeology and palaeontology remain the preserve of a minority, museums in Kenya have for the past few years been in the forefront of public education and heritage management. As opposed to the notion that museums are only galleries or houses for exhibition work, the National Museums of Kenya's activities are centred mainly on research, education and public services. It is important to look at the development of the research activities through time and the ways in which the system has been influenced by outside forces.

In Africa individual researchers have tended to dominate particular disciplines, including archaeology and palaeontology. They have, in many instances, adopted a regional outlook. As a result, certain people have become associated with all the research in a particular region. In some instances the monopoly has been so pronounced that one cannot talk of research in a particular region without mentioning the names of those concerned. For example, in Kenya as well as in Tanzania the Leakey family has been in the forefront of archaeological and palaeontological investigations since the 1920s. Their name has become associated not only with Olduvai Gorge and the Lake Turkana region (two of the areas known for evidence of early man) but also with the development of archaeology, palaeontology and museums in the two countries as a whole.

Another characteristic phenomenon in Kenya and Tanzania in particular has been the monopoly of these subjects by particular countries. A good example is in Kenya, where palaeolithic archaeology, palaeontological and geological studies have been dominated by North Americans; on the other hand, the neolithic, the Iron Age and historical archaeology have remained in the hands, mostly, of the British. At times groups or scholars of different opinions have even been in competition with each other. Such competition, however, has benefited only those who engaged in it.

In Kenya archaeology was not taught in schools as a subject. Even at university level it was not until the late 1970s that courses were started at the University of Nairobi. These courses, up to the present, still fall within the provinces of the History Department. In Kenya, and probably in most other African countries, the absence of these subjects in the school curriculum means that exposure to them is either through intermittent visits to museums with a school group or through history classes.

The National Museums of Kenya: origins

The idea of establishing a museum in Kenya was conceived on 25 March 1909, when ten people met at the house of the Lieutenant Governor, F. J. Jackson, for the purpose of considering the formation of a Natural History Society for East Africa. The outcome was to be the East Africa and Uganda Natural History Society. Part of its activities involved assembling scientific collections of natural history specimens. Of course, there was an obvious need for a museum to house and exhibit the specimens. By 1910 a room just big enough to accommodate the collected specimens had been provided in a house constructed next to the old Provincial Commissioner's Office in Nairobi. As more specimens came in, however, the room became too small to permit efficient cataloguing of the items collected.

In 1926 the society was given a site on which to erect a suitable building for its collections, on what used to be called Ainsworth Hill but is now known as Museum Hill. The new establishment was called the Carydon Memorial Museum; with the advent of independence it was renamed the National Museums of Kenya.

At present the National Museum in Nairobi receives about half a million visitors a year, about 350,000 of whom are local residents. Owing to the great need of funds to carry on various activities, overseas visitors are charged a fee, and there is a nominal fee for Kenya residents and school groups.

George H. O. Abungu

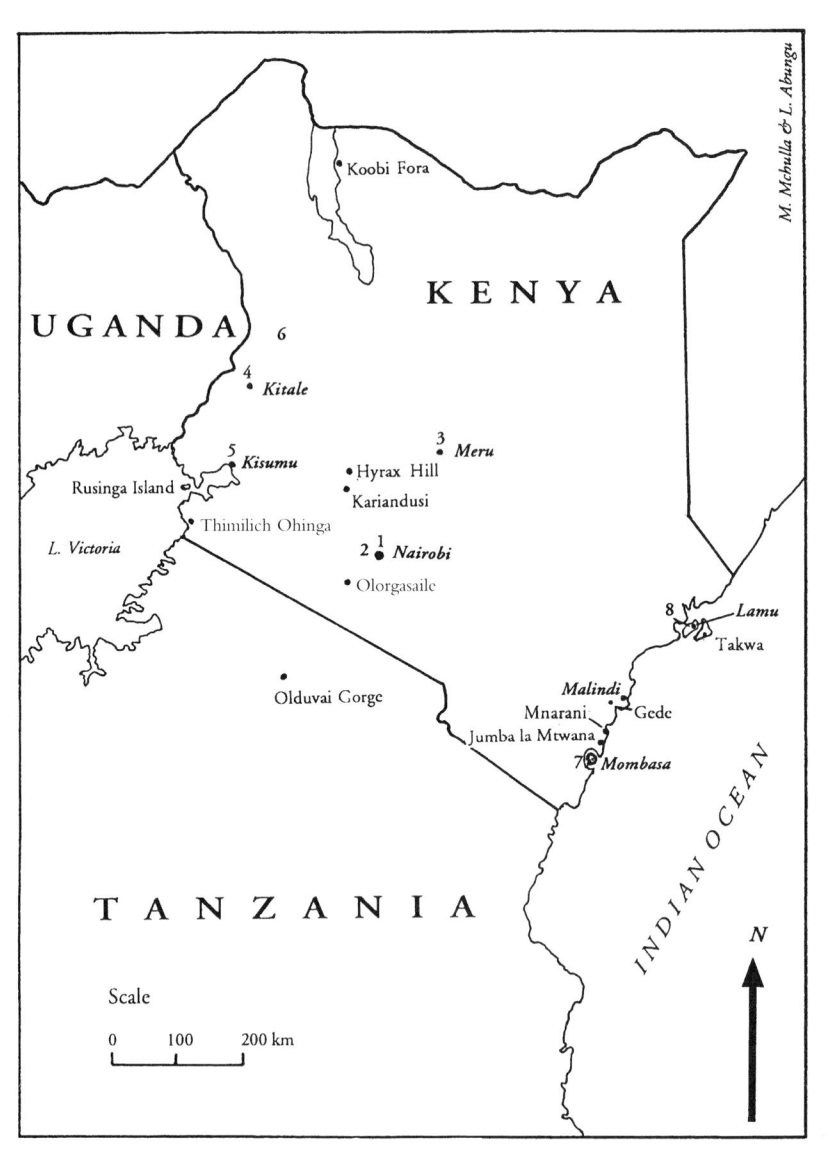

Map of Kenya showing major towns, sites and NMK Regional Museums

LEGEND   Regional Museums
1 Nairobi Museum
2 Karen Blixen Museum
3 Meru Museum
4 Kitale Museum
5 Kisumu Museum
6 Kapenguria Museum
7 Fort Jesus Museum
8 Lamu Museum
  Lamu Fort Environment Museum
  Lamu House Museum

site: Koobi Fora
town: *Mombasa*

144

Museum development

Since its foundation, the National Museums of Kenya have grown from a small family-like institution to a fully fledged museum with advanced research facilities. A number of extensions have been made to the museums, mostly through the setting up of special funds. Some of the additions include the new halls such as the Aga Khan Hall, built with funds donated by His Highness the Aga Khan. The greatest development of the National Museums, however, has come about in the last twenty-five years. The museum policy developed during this period concerned three main aspects, including:

1. The educational role of the museum in developing exhibits, within a broad educational programme, and providing services to schools, colleges and other institutions.

2. The provision of basic scientific services in the fields of reference, taxonomic study and identification, and the housing of scientific material essential to those services.

3. The development of international institutes in which Kenyans would actively participate, which would (primarily) serve as centres of excellence and which would benefit from overseas financial support and scientific collaboration.

Most of these aspects have been achieved, as collaboration work with other agencies and bodies has resulted in advanced scientific development. TILLMIAP (The International Louis Leakey Memorial Institute of African Prehistory) was established in 1977. It was followed by the Institute of Primate Research at Ololua and the Centre for Biodiversity at the National Museum of Kenya headquarters in Nairobi, among others. Most of the scientific divisions and departments are located at the National Museums' headquarters in Nairobi; there are, however, other regional museums which cater to a variety of aspects of museum activities.

Museum organization

As already mentioned, the Nairobi museum is the headquarters of all museum activities in Kenya. It is a unique institution, probably the only one of its kind in sub-Saharan Africa. The museum is not only known for its exhibits in the public galleries but has varied functions that fall broadly under the headings of preservation, research and education. These activities are categorized into divisions, which are further divided into departments. In total there are over twenty research departments in the museum. One example is the Natural Science Division, comprising the Departments of Zoology, Mammology, Herpetology, Ornithology and Entomology, which has existed since the inception of the National Museums of Kenya. However, (and perhaps unfortunately), most of the vital research activities of the various departments are rarely seen by the visitors to the public galleries.

The work of such divisions, like Natural Science, is not confined only to the museum. The division identifies and provides information on various species for other scientific institutions, government departments, the general public, researchers and educational institutions. It also undertakes the loan of teaching materials to schools. The division personnel also conduct research of a general taxonomic and ecological nature, the results of which are documented and kept as a national reference collection, apart from the work of curating such specimens. It is important to note that the research programmes of the National Museums of Kenya are far-ranging and include such fields as the development of contraceptives through primate research, the study of bilharzia and its treatment, and the origins of man (a field in which it has achieved international recognition), among others. The museum also provides research facilities for university students and other scholars, and is actively involved in the development of school curricula.

Regional museums and site museums

Regional museums were a concept that was developed to cater for the needs of the population in large towns far from Nairobi whose residents also required museum services. These museums, as such, were located in Kisumu, Kitale, Meru, Mombasa and Lamu. The main aim was the presentation of Kenya's cultural heritage, with special programmes for the preservation of the country's natural, cultural and architectural heritage.

To that end, the museum has brought under its protection a number of historically important sites such as Fort Jesus, Gede ruins, Takwa ruins, Olorgasaile, Rusinga Island in Lake Victoria, Koobi Fora in Lake Turkana and Thimilich Ohinga, an ancient stone village in south Nyanza. All are protected by the Antiquities and Monuments Act of 1983. There are many more sites but few are open to the public. The National Museums are therefore the primary institution entrusted with promoting a wide range of scientific and cultural activities in the country. The museum also remains the repository where all the fossils and artefacts are safely stored for research and reference.

Among the historical monuments along the coast is the famous Fort Jesus in Mombasa. This monument, which celebrated its four-hundredth anniversary recently, now houses a museum and serves as the administration and research headquarters of the coastal museums. The other coastal sites open to the public include Mbaraki, Jumba la Mtwana, Gede ruins, Mnarani ruins, the Vasco da Gama pillar in Malindi and the Takwa ruins in the Lamu archipelago.

In Lamu District are found the earliest archaeological remains of Swahili towns. In all, there are over 120 sites and monuments along the Kenyan coast alone, with the earliest settlements dating to the eighth century AD and found in the Lamu archipelago. Lamu Museum is located in the town of Lamu.

Most regional museums are more or less 'specialized' in different fields: the Lamu Museum represents material culture and local history; the Meru Museum focuses on cultural and agricultural development, with a special exhibit of live beekeeping; the Kisumu Museum illustrates cultural and natural history; while the Kitale Museum is similar in its content to the Nairobi Museum, with the general representation of natural sciences, prehistory, ethnography. This museum also has a good library.

Public resource management and the coastal museums

Fort Jesus Museum, in Mombasa, is slightly different from the other regional museums in that it houses a display of archaeological and cultural artefacts, as well as an exhibit of material from an underwater excavation which was carried out from 1978 to 1980. Within the fort, a conservation laboratory was established in response to the needs of this excavation of the wreck of a seventeenth-century frigate, the *San Antonio de Tanna*.

Figure 19.1a, b, c Views of the 'Palace' and 'Friday mosque' remains from the ancient Swahili town of Gede, now a site museum (*Photos: Lorna Abungu*)

Since the early 1980s, this laboratory has extended its responsibilities to the broader spectrum of archaeological preservation and conservation and can now reckon itself the best of its kind in the region. The laboratory deals with waterlogged and dry wood, leather and other organic materials, silver, brass, bronze, iron, coral lime, paper and cloth, among other things.

Recently the laboratory has offered training courses in conservation to

George H. O. Abungu

Figure 19.2 Lamu Museum: Lamu is the oldest inhabited town in Kenya and developed the first Old Town conservation programme
(*Photo: Lorna Abungu*)

Figure 19.3 Fort Jesus Museum Gallery: part of display hall showing archaeological and other materials
(*Photo: Lorna Abungu*)

museum staff of neighbouring countries, including Uganda, Tanzania, Zimbabwe and Zambia. Being the only laboratory of its kind in the region, it is now expanding and, it is to be hoped, will soon be training museum conservators from all over sub-Saharan Africa.

Fort Jesus also houses the National Museums of Kenya's Department of Coastal Archaeology, a research department that carries out archaeological

Figure 19.4 International students attached to the Department of Coastal Archaeology, engaged in excavation work at the Coast (*Photo: Lorna Abungu*)

surveys, excavation, documentation and analysis of archaeological material from all coastal settlements. The department is also entrusted with the conservation of all sites and monuments along the coast. Attached to the Department of Coastal Archaeology is the Regional Centre for the Study of Urban Origins in Eastern and Southern Africa. The centre is the result of a joint project between the National Museums of Kenya and the Swedish Agency for Research Co-operation with Developing Countries. Other countries involved in this project include Somalia, Tanzania, Comoro, Madagascar, Zimbabwe, Mozambique, Botswana and Namibia.

The centre possesses advanced research equipment and carries out desk-top publication. It produces a biannual newsletter, *MVITA*, used to discuss the research into urbanism carried out by scholars from the participating countries, and read by others who are interested in urban studies and African archaeology.

Another area that the coastal museums are engaged in, and more so for public benefit, is heritage conservation. Both the Fort Jesus and Lamu museums play the leading role in conservation work in their respective gazetted Old Towns.

Lamu, Kenya's oldest living town, is the centrepiece of the National Museums of Kenya's Building Conservation Programme. This programme has seen the rehabilitation of Lamu fort, where an Environment Museum is in the final stages of completion, and the improvement of the two public squares adjacent to the fort. A Conservation and Planning Office has also been established in order to implement the conservation programme. Within this office a project has been created, with assistance from the Ford Foundation, to train young apprentices in traditional building crafts (a key component of the museums' conservation effort).

Figure 19.5 (*left*) The ruined Pillar Mosque at the site of Takwa on the Lamu archipelago – now a site museum (*Photo: Lorna Abungu*)

Figure 19.6 (*right*) Fort Jesus Mombasa. Once a Portuguese garrison, the Fort is now a museum and serves as the headquarters for administration and research of the Coastal Museums (*Photo: Fort Jesus Collection*)

The Lamu conservation project is the first in the field of town conservation in Kenya. The project reflects Lamu's status as a remote and small, yet growing, urban community with a remarkably well preserved historical Old Town. In recent years rapid, uncontrolled development began to threaten the Old Town, which led to the current initiatives to protect the historical structures and promote careful and sympathetic development. Following a detailed study of the Old Town and the drafting of a comprehensive town conservation plan (including the enabling legislation, planning policies and design guidelines), Lamu was gazetted as an area of historical interest under the Antiquities and Monuments Act.

The Lamu fort, which had until recently been used as a prison, now contains maritime and environmental exhibits, the National Museums of Kenya's Centre for Building Conservation, houses Lamu's only public library, and includes a restaurant. This pioneering conservation work in Lamu has helped to spawn similar initiatives in the Old Town of Mombasa.

The Mombasa conservation project, which is under the care of Fort Jesus Museum, was conceived in November 1986 as a joint project of the United Nations Development Programme (the funding agency), UNESCO (the executing agency) and the National Museums of Kenya (the government implementing agency). This project, started in March 1987, aimed at preparing a conservation plan for Mombasa which would lay the groundwork of future town conservation and development.

Mombasa is unique. The inhabitants of its Old Town make up a richly diverse group of communities who have lived there side by side for hundreds of years. Their various social patterns, religions, economic activities and building traditions have created a distinct character and culture which together define the Old Town of Mombasa. Dated to the eleventh century through archaeological evidence, Mombasa has for centuries been the gateway to the interior of East Africa. The town's history and development are thus relevant not only to the people of the coast but to all Kenyans. As such, its conservation is important to the country and its people.

As in Lamu, the project is now being implemented and supervised by the National Museums of Kenya, which have formed an office called the Mombasa Old Town Conservation Office (MOTCO), situated in the Old Town, which monitors all new building developments. MOTCO's responsibilities include the following: assistance in monitoring construction activity within the conservation area; providing private developers, professionals and public officers with assistance and consultancy; helping with fund-raising campaigns; disseminating the conservation plan's philosophy (through seminars, educational campaigns, exhibits, videos, etc.); helping with the detailed preparation of schemes for the restoration and adaptation of historic buildings and for the improvement of public open spaces within the conservation area, among other things. In addition, an advisory board, the Mombasa Old Town Advisory Committee (the policy-making body), was formed for the promotion and development of the conservation effort. This body comprises three members each from the National Museums of Kenya, the municipal council of Mombasa and Old Town residents.

The activities of MOTCO are seen by the National Museums of Kenya as constituting a solid conservation approach to the planning and developing of communities. Such activities will be essential if communities are to remain livable urban centres as well as valuable cultural assets. Conservation here encompasses much more than just preserving monuments and old buildings; it means encouraging careful management of limited resources and promoting balanced growth and development. Through the activities of MOTCO and the other above-mentioned projects and programmes the National Museums of Kenya try to preserve the country's historic towns, their traditional skills and industries, and their cultural identity.

From the above it is obvious that the activities of the National Museums of Kenya cover a wide range of fields and have a strong public component. In this regard, such questions arise as:

1. How does the museum disseminate to the public the information it gathers from its research and other work?

2. Apart from the conservation and related work involving the public, especially along the coast, how do the National Museums of Kenya impart the message of the importance of such exercises?

3. In order for people to take part in museum-organized activities, how does the museum convince them of the value of these events?

Figure 19.7 Mbaraki Pillar: one of the landmarks in the historic city of Mombasa (*Photo: Lorna Abungu*)

Museums educating the public

Through the National Museums of Kenya, the government is encouraging the public to be aware of the importance of their historical, cultural and natural heritage. The museums are assisting the people to develop and sustain this pride, starting at primary school level. The museum's Department of Education has a series of programmes for schools, including subjects of topical as well as scientific interest. The popularity of the services is seen in

George H. O. Abungu

the rapid expansion of the department. It provides assistance to numerous schools and advises the regional museums on educational activities. The department runs a continuous series of lecture films, tours and courses at the museums, and in schools and colleges. These activities are of prime importance to general museum work.

Communicating with the public

The National Museums of Kenya employ all possible channels of mass communication to publicize their educational activities: television, radio, seminars, printed material, lectures and exhibitions. In all cases the National Museums of Kenya have been underscoring the fact that a museum's main functions are research, conservation and education. Through these activities the Kenyan museums, at a national level, receive more than 700,000 visitors per year. The Education Department of the museum is the main arm charged with the responsibility of disseminating information.

The department is planning to include in its annual programme a Museum Day on which admission will be free and museum work will be brought closer to the general public through hands-on learning in the various laboratories, mock excavations, etc. School competitions in art and essay writing, traditional dances, songs and poetry recitals will also act as communication links. Along the coast the department intends to highlight coastal archaeological sites along with marine environmental education during the museum's open days. In Lamu, the museum already hosts an annual dhow (traditional sewn boat) race and henna painting competition, events that are used to explain to the public the museum's activities. Further museum programmes will include simple publications and periodicals in the national language, KiSwahili.

Figure 19.8 (*left, below*) Mbarak Hinawy Street in the Old Town of Mombasa – note the intricately carved wooden verandah, now protected by an Act of Parliament
(*Photo: Motco Collection, Fort Jesus*)

Figure 19.9 (*right, below*) Dhow race in Lamu: one way of promoting cultural events through public participation in museum activities
(*Photo: Lorna Abungu*)

Figure 19.10 (*left*) The Mosque of Jumba la Mtwana, one of the site museums along the Kenya coast (*Photo: Lorna Abungu*)

Figure 19.11 (*right*) Fluted pillar tomb at the site of Shanga on Pate Island, Lamu Archipelago (*Photo: Lorna Abungu*)

Already, the Mombasa museum society, Friends of Fort Jesus, through slide lectures, video and film shows, and educational excursions, provides viable and rewarding communication with the different communities in town. In Nairobi the Education Department organizes a radio show known as 'Know your Museums' where various museum researchers have an opportunity to explain what their departments do. This gives the public the chance to learn more about what goes on behind the scenes, and will, hopefully, kindle more interest in the museums' varied activities.

Educational programmes for schools and students

Fort Jesus Museum's Education Department has been offering a variety of school programmes since its inception in 1975. The programmes focus on history and conservation. The school programmes focus on the museum displays, examining the history of Fort Jesus. The exhibition on the Portuguese shipwreck has a special significance in that it enlivens the history of the fort through the artefacts on display, which are a result of underwater archaeology. Other school programmes are based on the ethnography of coastal peoples, wildlife conservation, marine environmental education, and prehistory. Inter-school activities include essay and painting competitions, slide and video shows, and school outreach services.

Archaeology should, then, be a priority for museum education policy, since it is not included in the school curriculum. The reason given is that the system is already overloaded with subjects geared to lead directly to employment once students leave school, be it at primary, secondary or university level. Archaeology, it is argued, cannot contribute significantly to this goal.

The museum's role is to include the use of archaeological records to complement the history of the region as taught in schools, colleges and

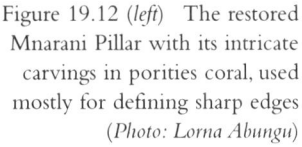

Figure 19.12 (*left*) The restored Mnarani Pillar with its intricate carvings in porities coral, used mostly for defining sharp edges (*Photo: Lorna Abungu*)

Figure 19.13 (*right*) Traditional dancers performing outside Fort Jesus as part of the cultural activities organized by the National Museums of Kenya (*Photo: B. Deiters*)

universities. It has to fill in where the curriculum is lacking. However, within the education departments of other institutions there is a shortage of suitable manpower and technology, which are needed to produce publications and other teaching aids effectively. Such things can be tools to highlight and promote the necessary subjects and activities among schoolchildren and the public. Education departments in our museums must therefore form a central part of our operations to inform and educate the public, and ensure that the museum's message is passed on.

The above reflects a weakness on the part of African governments and educational systems. While preaching cultural resource management they discourage the subjects through which it can be done. Our priorities do not allow the meagre resources available to be ploughed into cultural studies. It is therefore the responsibility of African museums not only to champion such studies but also to show that they are relevant and indispensable if any meaningful and positive development is to take place.

20 Nigeria
Museums in Archaeology Education

YASHIM ISA BITIYONG
Institute of Archaeology and Museum Studies, Jos

The primary message of federal government-owned museums in Nigeria at the start was to inform the public about the relevance of archaeological material in the historical experience of the people of Nigeria. However, the galleries have been accessible to only a small percentage of the population: largely those who live in the towns where the museums are located. Even in these centres strategies have not been effective enough to convince as many as the professionals would like that the museum and its archaeological exhibition are worth their time and effort.

Introduction

An attempt is made in this chapter to show that archaeological discoveries played a leading role in the establishment of the museum service in Nigeria. From the beginning, therefore, their essence was to educate Nigerians on the place of archaeological material in the historical experience of the people.

However, achievement of the noble goal of getting a large number of people so informed through exhibitions in the museum was limited. Only a small proportion of the population has visited the museums, mainly those who live in towns in which the museums are located. Thus in the case of the National Museum, Jos, non-archaeological, non-museum incentives had to be introduced to attract any meaningful number of visitors. The system of formal and informal education is partly responsible for the poor attitude to the museum and archaeological materials in particular. Publicity in the mass media is low and the syllabuses of the early school years do not contain sufficient archaeological information to stimulate a desire to learn more from the museum.

The National Commission for Museums and Monuments: emergence, early museums

Kenneth C. Murray was an art education officer and one of those who developed an interest in the preservation of antiquities during the colonial period. With him, E. H. Duckworth, also an officer in the Education Department, encouraged Nigerians and the government to adopt a systematic and scientific approach to the management of the country's material culture resources. They were inspired by the recovery of archaeological materials, the abundance of ethnographic materials and the proliferation of artworks in a variety of raw materials all over the country.

Yashim Isa Bitiyong

Figure 20.1 Excavation of a potsherd pavement at Ife

Emergence of the museum service and early museums

They sought the establishment of government-sponsored institutionalized structures for the documentation, preservation, publication and encouragement of the traditions of art in the country. They were particularly concerned about the rate of destruction and plunder of antiquities and monuments (Okita, 1985: 2–14): such incidents as the British plunder of Benin in 1897 and the excavations and export of antiquities from Ile-Ife by Frobenius in 1910/11, and the destruction of antiquities by the tin-mining activity of the Jos plateau which had come to light by 1928 and attracted the particular attention of Bernard Fagg, another enthusiast who was employed in the administrative service.

Okita notes that the untiring pressure of Duckworth and others for controlling legislation and museums was fired by what they viewed as the illicit export of archaeological objects (Okita, 1983: 6). As a result, a customs ordinance was issued in 1943. The same year an Antiquities Service was inaugurated. In 1945 an Antiquities Survey Unit was established in the Education Department. The unit was later moved to the Survey arm of the Works Department and has since moved in and out of several Ministries. The latest move was to the Federal Ministry of Information and Culture in 1991. A journal set up in 1933 was recognized as the official publication for the propagation and documentation of Nigerian culture. In 1954 an Antiquities Commission was established, following an enabling Antiquities Ordinance of 1953 which had sought to be more specific and all-embracing than the customs ordinance of 1943.

Museums were set up early at Esie, in Kwara State, at Ile-Ife, in Osun State, and at Jos, in Plateau State. Remarkable archaeological materials had been recovered from these areas. In Ile-Ife the brass, terracotta and potsherd

Figure 20.2 Preparations for excavations at Igbo Ukwu in 1959. 'Igbo Isaiah' with goat house and dividing compound wall removed. Excavations in this area revealed the famous 'storehouse of regalia' (*Photo: Thurstan Shaw Collection, University College London*)

pavement finds dug up by Leo Frobenius and by others after 1910/11 gave rise to what can be regarded as a site museum in the town. The purpose was to keep a record of the finds and to make them available for the education of the public. Similarly a site museum was established at Esie, where numerous stone figurines were found. And in Jos the same idea informed the establishment of what is now the National Museum in the capital of Plateau State. These early museums were therefore set up in response to the preservation and educational needs posed by archaeological finds. Where such major discoveries did not attract museums, as in the case of Igbo Ukwu, prominence has been given to the finds at the National Museum set up later in the former capital, Lagos (Okita, 1983: 6).

The National Commission for Museums and Monuments

The National Commission for Museums and Monuments was established in 1979, by decree No. 77 of the federal government. Up to 1979 the museums service was accorded only the status of a department directly controlled by the Ministry it came under. The parallel functioning advisory body on museum and monument matters appointed by government to give expert advice on policy had no control over the department. The 1979 law established a commission which brought the department and the advisory body together. It turned the advisory committee into a Governing Board which formulates and generally oversees policy implementation. A management team headed by a Director General supervises the commission's daily activities. It is, however, a low-grade commission which is placed in a Ministry rather than a priority grade commission located in the presidency and given direct funding.

Figure 20.3 Igbo Ukwu. A bronze roped pot, part of the 'storehouse of regalia' *in situ* at 'Igbo Isaiah'. The top of a globular pottery vessel and a bronze altar-stand can be seen in the background. (*Photo: Thurstan Shaw Collection, University College London*)

The commission is the agency of the federal government in charge of the administration of national museums, monuments and antiquities. It is the highest policy implementation organ, which is also responsible for the establishment and maintenance of national museums and other outlets related to the realm of antiquities, science, technology, warfare, arts, crafts, architecture, education and natural history.

In this way the commission's activities in the realm of archaeology, conservation, documentation and educational programmes, or those of its agents, are a matter of public concern. The public fund is the main source of sponsorship of the programmes. Provision has been made to enable the commission to seek out and to accept direct from the public gifts of antiquities, monuments, works of art, museums, land and money. Individuals may also be charged in money terms for services rendered. This means that by law and funding the organization has an obligation to the public and needs to fulfil it both in policy-making and in everyday implementation. Indeed, its history reflects this public service-oriented character, which owes much to the founders and their successors. But in this it manifests a weakness which runs through its operations. A strong bias towards the collection and exhibition of unique craft works characterizes the museums it runs, to the neglect of their contextual and environmental setting. The example of the National Museum, Jos, is unique and portrays the most comprehensive museum in the country, despite its limitations.

The National Museum, Jos

The example of the National Museum, Jos, demonstrates the relationship between archaeology and the museum, especially the way the commission has attempted to use archaeological materials in public education.

Museums in Archaeology Education

Figure 20.4 Igbo Ukwu in 1964 at the start of excavations (*Photo: Thurstan Shaw Collection, University College London*)

Following the observation of a consistent pattern of traits in finds recovered from the tinfields of central Nigeria on the Jemaa platform in the west of the Jos plateau, Bernard E. B. Fagg became convinced that he must move from his administrative position to the antiquity service, where he became Government Archaeologist. Building on the collection of archaeological materials already held by the Mines Department in Jos, he set up this museum in 1952. The gallery was dedicated particularly to the exhibition of finds of the Nok tradition which he had started publishing in the 1940s. Both the publications and the exhibition were aimed at public education on the finds. It was hoped that as a result the public in Britain would support colonial government expenditure on the antiquities service in Nigeria. It was also intended to arouse public awareness in Nigeria to the potential for the discovery of objects like those exhibited, in everyday activities, especially those that involved tilling the soil.

The response was encouraging and it spurred Fagg's research efforts. Many finds of terracotta, iron and stone objects were reported by mineworkers and by farmers who had visited or heard about the museum exhibits (Fagg, 1977). To date, villagers in the areas of old Jemaa (Gidan Waya) and Nok speak of the confidence in the activities of the archaeologist which they acquired from viewing the gallery or hearing about it, because it gave them assurance about what the archaeologist would use the collection for. There is a degree of competition in which each community hopes to have fine archaeological objects from their area on display in the gallery.

Many of these people, however, visited the museum because they were mineworkers. They had been encouraged to do so by their employers. Fagg had pleaded with the mine owners to support his efforts in that way. He also employed a few mineworkers to tour the minefields, exhibiting specimens at

159

Yashim Isa Bitiyong

Figure 20.5 Igbo Ukwu, 1964, 'Igbo Jonah' under excavation (*Photo: Thurstan Shaw Collection, University College London*)

hand, to discourage workers from destroying such finds, which they had come to believe were a bad omen. One such was Yusufu Potiskum, to whom credit is due for assisting in the recovery of many finds from the Jemaa/Nok core area of the Nok region. His was a rather special display of brilliance and dedication to duty in a one-man mobile mass education service of the museum (Fagg, 1977).

Attracting the public: additional activities and services

Visiting the exhibition was not sufficient encouragement alone. Avenues had to be created to draw the attention of the public to the museum's activities.

Tin-mining exhibition. In order to attract the mining community in and around Jos, and in recognition of the role of tin mining and the miners in the history of the museum, a tin-mining exhibition in a special gallery located away from the archaeology exhibition was established. It was aimed at encouraging movement around the premises. The exhibition gives briefings on the history, processing and uses of tin. It highlights the native and modern methods. An attempt is made to relate this to the history and economy of Jos.

Transport exhibition. In the area between the archaeology and tin-mining galleries a few specimens of some of the earliest motor vehicles used in northern Nigeria are on display in the open. Along with them is a small steam railway engine and coaches, relics of the railway system employed earlier in this century in the Jos area. The initial intention of keeping them in working order to provides rides around the museum has proved too ambitious yet.

Daily market. The transport exhibition occupies this open space with a daily open market square. A wing of the market has been provided for craft traders.

Pottery. The pottery section of the museum is located near by, where pottery of various types and sizes is produced for sale.

Museum of Traditional Nigerian Architecture. By the 1970s the museum had decided to broaden its focus. Interest had developed in the traditional architecture of Nigeria, for both its ethnographic and its technical potential. The Museum of Traditional Nigerian Architecture (MOTNA) project was started on the basis of studies conducted mostly in the 1960s. The aim was to construct replicas of pieces of the dying architectural traditions of the various parts of Nigeria on several hectares of land on the museum premises. Impressive in concept and execution, the replicas have attracted casual visitors but have also been used by architectural departments of universities for formal teaching purposes, and by the museum itself as office space and as exhibition galleries.

Other services. Also provided in these MOTNA pieces is provision for restaurant services. Other means by which the museum attracts visitors include letting out the auditorium, which is an edifice in modern Western style, organizing public lectures and the museum society. Special outings are arranged also.

The zoo. Perhaps the most successful of these public-attracting measures so far has been the establishment of a zoo in the museum complex. Visitation swelled thanks to the attraction of the animals. Matters were arranged so that a visit to the zoo had to be preceded by going to see the exhibit in the main gallery where the archaeological materials were displayed. A ticket to the Zoo was obtainable only at the end of the gallery visit. Now the policy has changed and the exhibition too. A visit to the gallery is no longer imposed. Nor is the zoo visit so exciting any longer, as the specimens have fallen in number and variety.

Thus even though a tradition has become established that literally thousands troop to the museum compound during Christian and Muslim festivities, they do so for the fun of picnicking rather than learning from the exhibitions. The visitors' book in the main gallery shows that expatriates are the main patrons of the exhibition. This means that the archaeological exhibits are seen by only a few Nigerians. The implications for the educational potentials of our archaeological finds are serious. It has been observed that the museum serves as the best forum by which archaeological materials can transmit their educational message and that this philosophy played a leading role in the establishment of the government museum tradition (Okita, 1983: 6–7).

This limitation notwithstanding, the National Museum, Jos, must stand out as a success story when considering Nigerian museums. Its location in a large metropolis, the erstwhile capital of the country, may have something to do with it, but no other museum in the country has attracted the visitors that this museum has. It stands out above Lagos in providing a variety of attractions other than the founding archaeological materials. The test of the quality of public education is seen in the fact that the museum has benefited from reports of many finds by people who have seen or heard of the museum's exhibitions and interest in such finds, thus buttressing archaeology's need for museum collaboration for public education about its finds.

Which strategies for outreach?

The Nigerian museum tradition has realized the need for effective collaboration with archaeology. This explains the inevitable emphasis on archaeological material in the museum galleries. By the 1970s a policy of establishing a Museum of National Unity in each state capital came into effect and the driving force of the museum setting ceased to be the discovery of archaeological materials. Archaeological objects remained the pride and occupied central place in the message of the museums that emerged in Benin, Kaduna, Kano, Maiduguri and Minna, for instance. The National Museum at the headquarters in Lagos displays such materials in proportionate abundance, which points to a status that befits its being the leading museum with the largest exhibition of archaeological finds from all over Nigeria. University museums in Ibadan, Nsukka, Port Harcourt and Zaria have shown the tendency to emphasize archaeological exhibits. And in the museums set up by the various Arts/Culture/History Councils/Bureaux across the country, archaeological finds get prominence. What we need in Nigerian museums now is strategies for outreach.

Need for a publicity drive

One of the guiding principles of such strategies must be to demonstrate any relevant linkage between the material evidence of the life of preceding, and perhaps ancestral, populations and present-day society; to emphasize the value of any recognizable societal strategies of problem-solving of the past to the modern situation. It seems that, given the Nigeria of today, by doing this the meaning of archaeological materials will be understood and enjoyed by the general public and not just by archaeologists and a few other professionals. Citizens may be able to devise new methods or techniques from this knowledge.

One specific instance may illustrate the point. During the last three years the National Commission for Museums and Monuments, through the Centre for Earth Construction Technology, Jos, in collaboration with the French Ministry of External Affairs and other French agencies, has launched a campaign to introduce to the public a technique of building construction in earth material for mass and individual housing. The campaign seeks to exploit traditional familiarity with the use of earth for house-building and to develop from it improved strategies for modern building construction. In this period, when housing construction materials are beyond the reach of most Nigerians, this marriage of old and new methods has received deserved public notice. The commission must link this programme with its other primary objectives. An exhibition showing old methods of earth construction, through its archaeological and ethnographic collection, linking up with the MOTNA project and the new methods, should educate the public on the relevance of archaeology and ethnographic research to the discovery of new methods. In this way the commission would be inviting the public to approach archaeological and other museum collections and other activities from the point of view of relevance. Perhaps architects, geologists and other specialists would see the place of archaeological collections in the chronology and promotion of their own professions.

The realization of the publicity requirement of the museum in a Third World country is not novel. One may only emphasize that the advertisement must be positive, and that the product must be relevant to the prospective customer. In 1970 Professor V. K. R. Rao, Education Minister of India, asked the museum to make a loud noise in order to be heard. He also asked us to persevere in seeking support and assistance for our programmes, even from the sponsoring Ministry (1970: 41).

Informal education

The programme of mass education must ensure that both rural and urban communities are reached. It is common knowledge that most of our archaeological finds are brought from rural areas. The analysis, storage, publication and exhibition are usually restricted to urban centres, by urban dwellers who have the power to take the decisions. This creates an urban bias, to the disadvantage of rural dwellers who hardly have an opportunity to view the exhibitions. The majority of them have no access to the published results because they cannot read in the languages of publication. This has informed calls for logistics to ensure rural participation in museum education programmes. Community museums and mobile exhibitions have been suggested, to complement each other. Some exhibitions satisfy specific local needs. Others may need to be taken to several localities at different times in accordance with a schedule. Government and private organizations at various levels – state and local as well as federal – should be involved in these efforts (Edet, 1990: 93–8; Okita, 1983: 7–8). The nearest the commission has come to establishing rural museums are the Esie site museum and the National Archaeological Museum of Nok Antiquities, at Kwoi, which has yet to acquire a gallery. The concept of mobile exhibitions appears to have died out. The vehicle used earlier in the exercise has broken down and appears too expensive to refurbish and run. Nigeria is large, and many such vehicles would be necessary to keep mobile exhibitions alive across the country.

The mass media

The mass media are available to be utilized in this museum endeavour. The number of daily newspapers and magazines is impressive. There is no less than one for each State, on average. This provides an opportunity for reaching out to the literate in rural and urban areas.

The radio appears to be a particularly relevant medium, with the largest audience, and has the advantage of transmitting in many languages. In each state there is a state government-owned radio station. Some have local sub-stations. The wide network of federal, state and local stations transmits daily for many hours. Given their policy of transmission in English and local languages, they constitute an important avenue.

Where television is available it has the advantage of both audio and visual perception. Nigeria is relatively well endowed here also. Each of the thirty states is served by at least one television station. Archaeology programmes were already being produced by professional broadcasters, for entertainment and general education. They are not yet available in Nigerian languages, however. Neither are they about Nigerian or other West African research. We need to work in this direction. The commission can solicit the co-operation of the television and radio authorities, the universities, the Information and Education Ministries, UNESCO, the West African Archaeological Association, the West African Museums Programme and the Archaeological Association of Nigeria.

Formal education   While dwelling this long on general informal education programmes, one is not oblivious of formal learning situations. Indeed, particular attention has been drawn to that sector by several scholars. They have decried the absence of archaeology education in the elementary and secondary school curriculum. This limitation appears, however, to be not just Nigerian but part of the underdevelopment phenomenon. Thus the calls for a solution by V. K. R. Rao (1970) in India, A. E. Afigbo (1985) in Nigeria, and by A. B. A. Adandé (1990) in Benin, point to the same problem. The setting is already being prepared for solution.

High-level education.   The tertiary level has started to offer students the opportunity to take a degree in archaeology. Set up in 1965, the programme at the University of Ibadan has matured into awarding several Ph.D. programmes. Ahmadu Bello University offers archaeology degrees as well as training technicians.

The Institute of Archaeology and Museum Studies, Jos, is a most important step in this direction. Started in 1963 as a UNESCO bilingual training centre, the Centre for Museum Studies in the National Museum, Jos, has grown into an Institute of Archaeology and Museum Studies. It comprises three centres: the Centre for Field Archaeology, the Centre for Museology and the Centre for Museum Studies. The first two offer postgraduate training and research, while the third offers training specifically in museum preservation and conservation.

The emergence of the institute in 1993 arose from recognition of the necessity for training and retraining cultural management personnel at both junior and senior level within the country. The two postgraduate centres had begun in 1990 as separate schools. One was in Jos while the other was located in Iffe Ijumu, Kogi State. However, both were soon brought together in Jos to use facilities and personnel jointly. This has also made it possible to expose the course participants to multidisciplinary training: archaeologists receive museology lectures while museologists become familiar with archeology. All the courses offered are oriented to practical work. The reason is that, in our universities, archaeologists are not equipped for project implementation. On the other hand, no first-degree programmes in museology are offered by the universities. This is why the commission has plans to establish a diploma-level course in the discipline, to provide further training for graduates of the existing Centre for Museum Studies course. The students of this institute are, in the main, employees of museums and related institutions from Nigeria and other African countries. It is hoped that in its new form it will provide an African base for researchers and graduate students from outside Africa, through specific affiliation programmes.

Secondary and primary schools.   The secondary and primary school levels require special attention. The opportunity arises in Nigeria through the Ministries of Education, which determine the course content at the elementary level. At the secondary school level the West African Examinations Council has the final say on the syllabus. These establishments need to be induced to infuse some archaeology into the syllabus. To get this done, archaeologists and other museum professionals must show interest and participate in the activities of the Examinations Council and the Education and other Ministries. And the efforts of the museum education unit must be reinvigorated in the area of school visits for talks, films and mobile exhibitions. This would enable us to educate pupils and policy-makers in those areas and to influence the changes.

Conclusion

The message seems to be that the abundance of archaeological material in the museums and the lessons they can teach will remain known only to a few museum professionals and a small proportion of the public unless the commission launches sustained aggressive and effective strategies to attract the large majority in both urban and rural areas to these. The commission is duty-bound.

References

Adandé, A. B. A. 1990. 'Cultural heritage, archaeology and education', in B. W. Andah (ed.), *Cultural Resource Management: an African dimension*. Ibadan: Wisdom Publishers.

Afigbo, A. E. 1985. 'History, archaeology and schools in Nigeria', in A. E. Afigbo and S. I. O. Okita (eds), *The Museum and Nation Building*. Owerri: New African Publishing.

Edet, A. 1990. 'Public archaeology and cultural resource management in Nigeria: resource conservation and development', in B. W. Andah (ed.), *Cultural Resource Management: an African dimension*. Ibadan: Wisdom Publishers.

Fagg, B. 1977. *Nok Terracotta*, London: Ethnographica.

Federal Military Government of Nigeria, National Commission for Museums and Monuments Decree 1979, Lagos.

Okita, S. I. O. 1983. 'The role of archaeological collections in cultural education in Nigeria', *Nigeria Magazine* 147, 1–10.

—— 1985, 'The emergence of public museums in Nigeria' in A. E. Afigbo and S. I. O. Okita (eds), *The Museum and Nation Building*. Owerri: New African Publishing.

Rao, V. K. R. V. 1970. 'Museums and the world of today: inaugural address', *ICOM News* 23 (4), 41–4.

Index

Abeke, 135
Abetifi, 3
Abidjan
   Musée national, xii, 24-8, 58, 121, 122, 123
   Université nationale de Côte d'Ivoire, 24, 26-8
   WAMP meeting (1993), ix, xii, xiv
Abomey, 127, 129
Abuja, 72
Académie des inscriptions et belles-lettres, Mali, 60
Accra National Museum (National Museum of Ghana), 3, 8-9, 11
Accra Plains Dangmeland, 5, 10
ACCT (Cultural and Technical Co-operation Agency), 112
Achimota College Museum, 3
Achimota farm, 3
Adandé, A.B.A., 164
AEEM (Association des Élèves et Étudiants du Mali), 116
Afigbo, A.E., 164
Afikpo, 38, 39
Afik-speaking areas, 39
Agadez, 95
Aga Khan, 145
Ahmadu Bello University, 19, 164
Aïr area, Niger, 95, 96
Aïr Ténéré, Niger, 97
Akuapem, 3
Akumbu tell site, *63*
Alboury, Bouna, 89, *90*
Allada, artefacts from, *50*

Amis de Djenné, 64
Antiquities Commission, Nigeria, 69-70, 156
Archaeological Association of Nigeria, 75, 164
Arcotech, 104
Association des Élèves et Étudiants du Mali (AEEM), 116
Association malienne pour la promotion sociale des aveugles (Malian Association for the Social Advancement of the Blind), 112, 114
Association of Wholly or Partially French-speaking Universities (AUPELF), 45
Atlantic, 84, 100
Azawak area, 95

Bakel, 88
Bakhadiakh marigot, 84
Bamako
   IFAN Centre, 60
   Institut des sciences humaines (ISH), 61, 62, 65, 66, 111, 113
   Musée national du Mali, 61, 62, 111-9
Bandiagara escarpment, 61
Bargny, 83
Bargny-Est plateau, 84
Begho, 5
   brass bowl from, *10*
   burial, *8*
   geodetic survey, *9*
Béké, 135

Index

Benin
   Béninois Archaeological Research Team (Equipe de recherche archéologique béninoise; ERAB), 44, 47, 49
   Centre d'activités éducatives du Bénin, 129
   comunication and education, 125-33
   Directorate of the Cultural Heritage, 47, 127, 129
   Historical Archaeology Project, 45
   Musée ethnographique (Porto Novo), 47, 48, *49*
   Musée Honmè, 129
   training in archaeology, 44-51
   Université du Bénin (Togo), 45
   Université nationale du Bénin, 44-51, 127, 129
Benin, Nigeria, 12, 156, 162
Benue, Cameroon, 135
Benue project, Nigeria, 21
Bidojato
   site, *128*
   stone heads from, *127*
Bidzar, 134
Bingerville, 122
Biti, 135
   shaft at, *138*
   stone tools from, *137*
Bocar, Sada, 89
Bolgatanga regional museum, 5, 8
Bondoukou, 122
Bosumpra cave, 3
Botswana, 149
Bougouni region: terracotta tortoise from, *116*
British, 11, 12, 13, 143, 159
Bulletin de l'IFAN, 60
Bundu, 89
Burkina Faso
   'Archéologie au Burkina Faso' exhibition, 107
   Centre national de la recherche scientifique et technique (CNRST), 79
   Centre voltaïque de la recherche scientifique (CVRS), 77
   Club d'histoire Cheikh Anta Diop, 78
   communication and education, 107-110
   Directorate of the Cultural Heritage, 79, 80
   Georges Melliès French Cultural Centre, 78
   History and Archaeology Club, 107
   IFAN in, 77, 79
   'La porterie dans la société traditionelle burkinabé' exhibition, 107
   legislation, 79-80
   Maison de la Presse Mohamed Maïga, 78
   management of the archaeological heritage, 77-80
   Ministry of Culture, 78, 79, 80
   Ministry of Secondary and Higher Education and Scientific Research, 78, 79
   Musée national, 77, 78, 79, 107, 109, 110
   Museum Department, 79
   National Assembly of Upper Volta, 77
   Pobé Mengao village museum, 108-9
   Université de Ouagadougou, 45, 51, 77-8, 79, 80, 107, 108

CAFAC (Centre d'animation et de formation à l'action Culturelle), Côte d'Ivoire, 25
California: University of California at Los Angeles (UCLA), 45
Cameroon
   archaeological research in, 134-6
   teaching and transmission of archaeology in Museum of Cameroon, 134-41
Cape Verde
   legislation, 98-9
   National Cultural Institute (INAC), 98, 102, 103, 104
   National Museum of Cultural History proposed, 98
   site and archaeological heritage conservation at Cidade Velha, 98-104

Cape Verde promontory, Senegal, 83-4
  pottery from, *84*
Cap Manuel, 83
Carabane, 88
Caritas, 101
Carthage, 95
Carydon Memorial Museum (later National Museums), Nairobi, 143
  see also National Museums of Kenya
Casamance, 88
Casamance, River, 85
Cassard, Jacques, 100
Central Sahara area: fragment of silicified wood, *50*
Centre d'activités éducatives du Bénin, 129
Centre d'animation et de formation à l'action Culturelle (CAFAC), Côte d'Ivoire, 25
Centre de recherches sur les arts et la culture, Côte d'Ivoire, 57
Centre for Earth Construction Technology, Jos, 162
Centre for Field Archaeology, Jos, 164
Centre for Museology, Jos, 164
Centre for Museum Studies, Jos, 164
Centre for Preventative Conservation in Tropical Africa (PREMA), 73
Centre for Training Museum Technicians, Nigeria, 73
Centre national de la recherche scientifique et technique (CNRST), Burkina Faso, 79
Centre national de recherches en sciences humaines, Niger, 94
Centre nigérien de recherches en sciences humaines (CNRSH), Niger, 95
Centre voltaïque de la recherche scientifique (CVRS), 77
Chad, Lake, 135
Cidade Velha (formerly Ribeira Grande)
  archaeologcal heritage conservation, 98-104
  Cathedral, *101*, 101-2
  Church of Mercy, *102*, 102
  Church of Our Lady of Rosario, *102*
  City Gate, 102
  Fort of S. Verissimo, 102
  history, 99-101
  remains of walls, *100*
  Royal Fort of St. Philip, *103*
  site museum project, 101-4
  view of, *99*
Club d'histoire Cheikh Anta Diop, 78
CNRSH (Centre nigérien de recherches en sciences humaines), Niger, 95
CNRST (Centre national de la recherche scientifique et technique), Burkina Faso, 79
Cocotomey, artefacts from, *50*
communication and education, xi, 107-65
  in Benin, 125-33
  in Burkina Faso, 107-110
  in Cameroon, 134-41
  in Côte d'Ivoire, 120-124
  in Kenya, 142-54
  in Mali, 111-9
  in Nigeria, 155-65
Comoro, 149
Côte d'Ivoire
  archaeological training, 24-8
  Centre d'animation et de formation à l'action Culturelle (CAFAC), 25
  Centre de recherches sur les arts et la culture, 57
  communication and education, 120-124
  Directorate for the Promotion of the Cultural Heritage, xiv, 55
  Ecole de formation à l'action Culturelle (EFAC), 25
  history books, 121, 123
  IES, 57
  Institut d'histoire, d'art et d'archéologie africains (IHAAA), xii, 26, 55, 57, 58, 121
  legislation, 56
  management of the cultural heritage, 55-8
  Ministry of Culture, xiv, 57, 58, 121
  Ministry of National Education, 123
  Musée national, Abidjan, xii, 24-8, 58, 121, 122, 123

Index

private museums, 121
Université nationale de Côte d'Ivoire, 24, 26-8
Cultural and Technical Co-operation Agency (ACCT), 112
curator, responsibilities of, 16-17
CVRS (Centre voltaïque de la recherche scientifique), 77

Dagana, 88
Dahomey, Université du, 44
Daima, 12
    excavation trench, *13*
Dakar
    Institut français de l'Afrique noire (IFAN), 60, 77, 95
    journals published in, 60
    stone lyre in, 86, *87*
    Université de (Université Cheikh Anta Diop), 31-2, 82, 90, 91, 92
    mentioned, 83, 89
Dakar-Hann, Neolithic pottery from, *84*
Dangme potter, 7
David, N., 134-5
Dawu, 3
Dékhelé, 89
Delbi, 86
Deni-Youssouf ravine, 84
Desplagnes, L. 60
Devisse, Professor Jean, 44, 120
Diack, 83
Diakhao, 89
Diakhité, 83, *84*
Diallowali, 89
Diama dam, 83, 86
Dionewar: shell midden, *85*
Divo, 122
Djado, 96
Djenné (*see* Jenné)
Dogo, 61
Dogon, 108
Drake, Francis, 100
Duckworth, E.H., 155, 156
Dutch, 10
Dutsen Kongba, 72

East Africa, 142, 151
East Africa and Uganda Natural History Society, 143
Ecole de formation à l'action Culturelle (EFAC), Côte d'Ivoire, 25
education *see* communication and education
El Oualadji, 60
Eleru rock shelter, *13*
Elmina, 5, 10
English, 100
Enugu, 42
Equipe de recherche archéologique béninoise (ERAB; Béninois Archaeological Research Team;), 44, 47, 49
Esie Museum, 71, 156, 157, 163
Essomba J.M., 135
Ezira, 38, 39

Faboura, 85
Fagg, Bernard E.B , 71, 72, 156, 159
Fakola, terracotta statuette from, *118*
Falémé, River, 83
Fana, 111
Fanfannyègèné, 62, 113
Ford Foundation, 149
Fort Jesus Museum, 146-9, 150, *150*, 153
    display hall, *148*
    performance outside, *154*
French, 59, 77, 87, 100-101, 162
French Ministry of External Affairs, 162
Frobenius, Leo, 156, 157
Fuladu, 89
Fulbe, 108

Gado, Boube, 96
Gambia, River, 85
Gede ruins, 146
    'Palace' and 'Friday mosque' remains, *147*
Georges Melliès French Cultural Centre, Burkina Faso, 78
Gérard, Bertrand, 108
Ghana
    Ghana Museums and Monuments Board (GMMB), 4, 5, 9, 11
    monuments and archaeology in, 10-11

Index

museum and archaeology training at University of Ghana, Legon, 3-11
National Museum, Accra, 3, 8-9, 11
GMMB (Ghana Museums and Monuments Board), 4, 5, 9, 11
Gohitafla, 57, 122
Gorée, 87, 89
Guédé, 89
Guinea region, 21

Hamdallahi, 89
Hamdallaye, 89
Hartle, Donald D., 37, 38-9, 40
Hartle, Janet, 38
Haute Vallée, 66
heritage, definition of, 55-6, 68-9
see also management of the archaeological heritage
Hervieu, J., 134
Historical Archaeology Project, Benin, 45
Ho, 5, 8
Honmè, 129
Houngbanou, artefacts from, 50

Ibadan, University of, 12-23, 45, 72, 162, 164
ICMAH (International Committee on the Management of the Archaeological Heritage), 68-9
ICOM (International Council of Museums), ix, 15
Ifa shrine, Ijesha Palace, 20
IFAN (Institut français/fondamental d'Afrique noire), 25, 60, 77, 79, 82, 86, 90, 94, 111
IFAN-Ch. A. Diop, 90, 91, 92
Ife see Ile-Ife
Ifeka Garden bronzes, 38
Iffe Ijumu, 164
Igall-Teggiden'Tessum region, 95
Igbo, 38, 39
Igbo Ukwu, 12, 157, *159*
 bronze roped pot, *158*
 'Igbo Isaiah' excavation, *157*
 'Igbo Jonah' excavation, *160*
IHAAA (Institut d'histoire, d'art et d'archéologie africains), Côte d'Ivoire, xii, 26, 55, 57, 58, 121

Ijesha Palace
 Ifa shrine, *20*
 Palace complex, *19*
 Sampono (Olode's) shrine, *20*
Ikoku, Professor Chimere, 37
Ile-Ife
 Museum, 71, 156-7
 potsherd pavement, *156*
INAC (National Cultural Institute), Cape Verde, 98, 102, 103, 104
Institut de recherches en sciences humaines (IRSH), Université de Niamey, 95
Institut des sciences humaines (ISH), Mali, 61, 62, 65, 66, 111, 113
Institut d'histoire, d'art et d'archéologie africains (IHAAA), Côte d'Ivoire, xii, 26, 55, 57, 58, 121
Institute of Archaeology and Museum Studies, Jos, 73, 164
Institute of Primate Research, Ololua, 145
Institut fondamental d'Afrique noire, Niger, 94
Institut fondamental d'Afrique noire, Senegal, 31, 82, 90
Institut français d'Afrique noire see IFAN
International Committee on the Management of the Archaeological Heritage (ICMAH), 68-9
International Council of Museums (ICOM), ix, 15
International Institute of Tropical Agriculture, 21
International Louis Leakey Memorial Institute of African Prehistory (TILLMIAP), 145
Iron Age, 10, 84-7, 135
IRSH (Institut de recherches en sciences humaines), Université de Niamey, 95
ISH (Institut des sciences humaines), Mali, 61, 62, 65, 66, 111, 113
Isienu, 42
Iwo Eleru, 12
 Iwo Eleru Man, *13*

171

Index

Jackson, F. J., Lieutenant Governor of Kenya, 143
Jemaa platform, 159, 160
Jenné region, 61, 63-4, 66
    terracotta head from, *118*
    see also Jenné-Jeno
Jenné-Jeno, 63, 64, 66
    jar inhumation from, *65*
    large exposure (LX), *64*
    terracotta figures from, *61, 62*
Jos
    Centre for Earth Construction Technology, 162
    Centre for Field Archaeology, 164
    Centre for Museology, 164
    Centre for Museum Studies, 164
    Institute of Archaeology and Museum Studies, 73, 164
    Museum, 7, 68-76, 155, 156, 157, 158-61, 164
    tin mining, 71, 156, 160
Jumba la Mtwana, 146
    Mosque, *153*

Kaduna, 162
Kano, 162
Kaolack, 85, 86, 87
Karkarichinkat, 61
Kati, 111
Katsina-Ala, Nok terracotta head from, *74*
Kawar, 96
Kenya, National Museums of, 142-54
    Building Conservation Programme, 149
    Centre for Biodiversity, 145
    Centre for Building Conservation, 150
    communicating with the public, 152-3
    Department of Coastal Archaeology, 148-9
    development of, 145
    educational programmes for schools and students, 153-4
    Education Department, 151-2, 153, 154
    map, *144*

museum organization, 145-6
origins of, 143
Regional Centre for the Study of Urban Origins in Eastern and Southern Africa, 149
regional museums and site museums, 146
role in educating the public, 151-2
Keur Ali Laobé, 86
Khant site, 83
Kiéthéga, Jean-Baptiste, 77
Kili, 60
Kipre, Pierre, 121
Kisumu Museum, 146
Kitale Museum, 146
Koma-Bulsa burial mounds
    excavation, *4*
    terracotta sculptures from, *5, 6*
Komaland project, 5
Koobi Fora, 146
Koumbi Saleh, 60
Koumpetoum: megalithic circle, *88*
Kounoune, 84
Kourounkorokalé, 65, *67*
Kumasi, 8
Kurumba, 108, 109
Kurumfe, 108
Kwahu, 3
Kwoi: National Archaeological Museum of Nok Antiquities, 163

Labouret, 60
Lagos
    Federal Department of Antiquities transferred to, 72
    National Museum, 12, 157, 162
    University of, 38
Lampsar, 88
Lamu
    Conservation and Planning Office, 149
    conservation programme, 149-50
    dhow race, *152*, 152
    fort, 149, 150
    Museum, 146, *148*, 152
    Old Town, 150
Lamu archipelago, sites in, 146, *150*, 153
Leakey family, 143

Lebeuf, Jean-Paul and Annie, 135
Legon: University of Ghana, 3-11
Leija, 42
Lomé: WAMP colloquium (1985), ix
London University Institute of Archaeology, 7
Lorum, 108, 109
Loucou, Jean Noël, 121
Loumpet, Alexandra and Germain, 135

Maboumba, 89
McDonald, Kevin, 63
Macina, terracotta bedpost from, *118*
McIntoshes, 63, 64
Madagascar, 149
Maiduguri, 162
Maison de la Presse Mohamed Maïga, Burkina Faso, 78
Maka Gouye, 86
Mali
  Académie des inscriptions et belles-lettres, 60
  Association des Élèves et Étudiants du Mali (AEEM), 116
  Association malienne pour la promotion sociale des aveugles, 112, 114
  colonial era, 59-60
  communication and education, 111-9
  current trends in archaeology, 61-63
  Division of the Cultural Heritage of Mali, 64
  IFAN in, 60, 111
  Institut des sciences humaines (ISH), 61, 62, 65, 66, 111, 113
  management of the archaeological heritage, 59-67
  Ministry of Culture and Communication, 111
  Ministry of National Education, 111
  Ministry of Youth, Sport, Arts and Culture, 111, 115
  Museé national du Mali, 61, 62, 111-9
  Museé soudanais, 111
  Opération aménagement et production forestière (OAPF), 65
Malindi: Vasco da Gama pillar, 146
Mamelles, 83
management of the archaeological heritage, xiii, 55-104
  in Burkina Faso, 77-80
  in Cape Verde, 98-104
  in Côte d'Ivoire, 55-8
  in Mali 59-67
  in Niger, 94-7
  in Nigeria, 68-76
  in Senegal, 81-93
Manding mountains, 64-6, *66*
Maret, Pierre de, 135
Markala burial site, *117*
Marliac, Alain, 134
Matam, 89
Mauritania, 31
Mayo Kedi, 135
Mbaraki, 146
  Mbaraki Pillar, Mombasa, *151*
Mbi, 135
Medeiros, François de, 44
Médina Wouro, 89
Méma, 63
Mérinaghene, 88
Meru Museum, 146
Mezières, Bonnel de, 60
Minna, 162
Mnarani
  Pillar, *154*
  ruins, 146
Molo, Alpha, 89
Molo, Mousssa, 89
Mombasa
  conservation project, 150-1
  Fort Jesus Museum, 146-9, 150, *150*, 153, *154*
  Mbarak Hinawy Street, *152*
  Mbaraki Pillar, *151*
  Mombasa Old Town Advisory Committee, 151
  Mombasa Old Town Conservation Office (MOTCO), 151
Mono valley, 45
Montallet, Jacques, 135
Moose, 108
Moru-Zakpé, artefacts from, *50*

Index

MOTCO (Mombasa Old Town Conservation Office), 151
MOTNA (Museum of Traditional Nigerian Architecture) project, 161, 162
Mozambique, 149
Murray, Kenneth C., 155
Musée d'histoire naturelle, Paris, 95
Musée de l'homme, Paris, 95
Musée du Bardo (Tunis), 112
Musée ethnographique (Porto Novo), 47, 48, *49*
Musée Honmè, 129
Musée national, Burkina Faso, 77, 78, 79, 107, 109, 110
Musée national, Côte d'Ivoire, xii, 24-8, 58, 121, 122, 123
Musée national des arts africains et océaniens, Paris, 79, 86
Musée national du Mali, 61, 62, 111-9
Musée national du Niger, 94-7
Musée soudanais, Mali, 111
museography, 33-6
Museum of Cameroon, 134-41
Museum of National Unity policy, Nigeria, 162
Museum of Traditional Nigerian Architecture (MOTNA) project, 161, 162
museums, role of, 15-16, 24-5, 125-7, 142 *see also* names of museums
Muslims, 33, 56, 109
MVITA (newsletter), 149

Nairobi: National Museum, 143, 145-6, 153
Namibia, 149
Nassarao II, 135
National Archaeological Museum of Nok Antiquities, Kwoi, 163
National Assembly of Upper Volta, 77
National Commission for Museums and Monuments (NCCM), Nigeria, 42, 68-76, 157-8, 162
National Cultural Institute (INAC), Cape Verde, 98, 102, 103,104
National Museum, Jos, Nigeria, 7, 68-76, 155, 156, 157, 158-61, 164

National Museum, Lagos, Nigeria, 12, 157, 162
National Museum of Cultural History, Cape Verde, proposal for, 98
National Museum of Ghana, Accra, 3, 8-9, 11
National Museums of Kenya, 142-54
NCCM (National Commission for Museums and Monuments), Nigeria, 42, 68-76, 157-8, 162
Nda Akoa II rock shelter, *139,140*
Ndalane, 87
Ndindan, 135
Ndoffène, Bour Sine Coumba, 89
Ndorma, 89
Ngol Ngol, 89
Ngor, 89
Niamey
  Institut de recherches en sciences humaines (IRSH), 95
  Musée national du Niger, 94-7
  Niamey Institut régional de muséologie, 96
  Université de, 95, 96
Niger
  Centre national de recherches en sciences humaines, 94
  Centre nigérien de recherches en sciences humaines (CNRSH), 95
  IFAN centre, 94, 95
  Institut de recherches en sciences humaines (IRSH), Université de Niamey, 95
  Institut fondamental d'Afrique noire, 94
  legal and institutional problems, 96-7
  management of the archaeological heritage, 94-7
  Ministry of Communication, Culture, Youth and Sport, 94, 97
  Ministry of the Interior, 97
  Ministry responsible for higher education and research, 97
  Musée national du Niger, Niamey, 94-7
  ORSTOM, 95, 96
Niger, inland delta of the, 61, 64

Niger valley, 96
Nigeria
  Ahmadu Bello University, 19, 164
  Antiquities Commission, 69-70, 156
  Antiquities Ordnance (1953), 69-70, 156
  Antiquities (Prohibited Transfer) Decree No. 9 (1974), 70
  Antiquities Survey Unit, 156
  Archaeological Association of Nigeria, 75, 164
  Centre for Earth Construction Technology, Jos, 162
  Centre for Field Archaeology, Jos, 164
  Centre for Museology, Jos, 164
  Centre for Museum Studies, Jos, 164
  Centre for Preventative Conservation in Tropical Africa (PREMA), 73
  Centre for Training Museum Technicians, 73
  civil war, 38
  communication and education in relation to museums, 155-65
  Councils for Arts and Culture, 71, 72
  Decree No. 77 (1979), 70, 74, 157
  Department of Mines, 71, 159
  Directorate of Rural Development and Infrastructure, 19
  Education Department, 155, 156
  Esie Museum, 71, 156, 157, 163
  Federal Department of Antiquities, 69, 70, 72
  Federal Ministry of Information and Culture, 156
  Ile-Ife Museum, 71, 156-7
  Institute of Archaeology and Museum Studies, 73, 164
  Jos museum, 7, 68-76, 155, 156, 157, 158-61, 164
  legislation, 69-70, 74, 156, 157
  management of the archaeological heritage, 68-76
  mass media, 163-4
  Ministries of Education, 165
  Museum of National Unity policy, 162
  Museum of Traditional Nigerian Architecture (MOTNA) project, 161, 162
  National Archaeological Museum of Nok Antiquities, Kwoi, 163
  National Commission for Museums and Monuments (NCMM), 42, 68-76, 157-8, 162
  National Museum, Jos, 7, 68-76, 155, 156, 157, 158-61, 164
  National Museum, Lagos, 12, 157, 162
  Nigeria-Biafra war, 38
  Nigerian Antiquities Service, 69, 72, 156
  permits for archaeological work, 69-70, 70-1, 75
  training in museums and archaeology, 12-23, 37-43
  University of Lagos, 38
  University of Ibadan, *12*, 12-23, 72, 162, 164
  University of Nigeria, Nsukka, 19, 37-43, 72, 162
  Works Department, 156
Njenawat, 83, 84
Nkometu, 135
Nok culture, 73, 159
  terracotta heads, *72*, *74*
Nok region, 72, 159, 160
North Americans, 143
Notes africaines, 60
Nouakchott: WAAA colloquium (1984), ix
Nsukka: University of Nigeria, 19, 37-43, 72, 162
Nyanza, 146
Nyorosa, 108

OAPF (Opération aménagement et production forestière), Mali, 65
Obobogo, 135
Obukpa, 39
Odoh, Godwin, 39
Ogbodu Aba, 42
Okita, S.I.O., 156
Okolo, 135
Old Kafanchan: Nok terracotta, *72*

Index

Olduvai Gorge, 143
Oliga, 135
Ololua: Institute of Primate Research, 145
Olorgasaile, 146
Opération aménagement et production forestière (OAPF), Mali, 65
Opi slag shrines, *22*
ORSTOM, 95, 96
Ouagadougou
    IFAN centre, 77
    Musée national, 77, 78, 79, 107, 109, 110
    Université de, 45, 51, 77-8, 79, 80, 107, 108
    West African Archaeological Association fifth colloquium (1992), ix, 47, 49
Ouessè, 45, 127
    pottery from, *131*, *132*
Ouidah, 45, 127, 129

Parc du W, Niger, 97
Paris
    Musée de l'homme, 95
    Musée d'histoire naturelle, 95
    Musée national des arts africains et océaniens, 79, 86
    Université de Paris I, 44
    Université de Paris IV, 55
Paris, François, 96
Pate Island: pillar tomb, *153*
Petite Côte, 83
Philippe, Professor Bruno, 55
Pire, 89
Pleistocene era, 135, 136
Pobé Mengao village museum, 108-9
Podor, 86, 89
Pointe des Almadies, 89
Port Harcourt, 162
Porto Novo
    Musée ethnographique, 47, 48, *49*
    Musée Honmè, 129
    mentioned, 127
Portuguese, 99, 100, 101, 102, 153
Potiskum, Yusufu, 160
Praia, 98, 101, 103, 104

PREMA (Centre for Preventative Conservation in Tropical Africa), 73

Quaternary, 32, 136

Rao, 87
Rao, Professor V.K.R., 163, 164
Regional Centre for the Study of Urban Origins in Eastern and Southern Africa, 149
Retba, Lake, 84
Ribeira Grande *see* Cidade Velha
Richard Toll, 89
Roger, Baron, 89
Rop rock shelter, *75*
Roset, Jean-Pierre, 96
Rufisque, 83, 84, 89
Rusinga Island, 146

St Jago fort, 10-11
Saint-Louis, 83, 87, 89
Saloum islands: shell midden, *85*
Sampona (Olode's) shrine, Ijesha Palace, *20*
San Antonio de Tanna wreck, 146
Santiago, 99
Sao area, 135, *136*
Savi, 45, *48*
    paving, *46*
Sébikotane
    chert found near, 83
    Old Stone Age site, *30*
    William Ponty School, 89, *91*
Sédhiou, 89
Senegal
    Bureau of Architecture and Historic Monuments, 90
    Commission supérieure des monuments historiques, 81, 90, 91, 92
    Directorate of the Historic and Ethnographic Heritage, 81, 82, 86, 90
    Directorate of Tourism Promotion, 91
    historic sites, 87-9
    Institut fondamental d'Afrique noire 31, 82, 90